DANIEL KORSCHUN & GRANT WELKER

WE ARE MARKET BASKET

THE STORY OF THE UNLIKELY GRASSROOTS MOVEMENT THAT SAVED A BELOVED BUSINESS

AMACOM

AMERICAN MANAGEMENT ASSOCIATION
NEW YORK • ATLANTA • BRUSSELS • CHICAGO • MEXICO CITY •
SAN FRANCISCO • SHANGHAI • TOKYO • TORONTO • WASHINGTON, D.C.

Bulk discounts available. For details visit:
www.amacombooks.org/go/specialsales
Or contact special sales:
Phone: 800-250-5308
Email: specialsls@amanet.org
View all the AMACOM titles at: www.amacombooks.org

This publication is designed to provide accurate and authoritative information in regard to the subject matter covered. It is sold with the understanding that the publisher is not engaged in rendering legal, accounting, or other professional service. If legal advice or other expert assistance is required, the services of a competent professional person should be sought.

Library of Congress Cataloging-in-Publication Data

Korschun, Daniel.
    We are Market Basket : the story of the unlikely grassroots movement that saved a beloved business / Daniel Korschun and Grant Welker.
        pages cm
    Includes bibliographical references and index.
    ISBN 978-0-8144-3665-3 (hardcover)—ISBN 0-8144-3665-X (hardcover)—ISBN 978-0-8144-3668-4 (ebook)
    1. Market Basket (Firm) 2. Supermarkets—United States—Management. 3. Grocery trade—United States—Management. 4. Corporate governance—United States—Case studies. I. Welker, Grant. II. Title.
    HF5469.23.U64M375 2015
    381'.45641309744—dc23   2015006561

About AMA
American Management Association (www.amanet.org) is a world leader in talent development, advancing the skills of individuals to drive business success. Our mission is to support the goals of individuals and organizations through a complete range of products and services, including classroom and virtual seminars, webcasts, webinars, podcasts, conferences, corporate and government solutions, business books and research. AMA's approach to improving performance combines experiential learning—learning through doing—with opportunities for ongoing professional growth at every step of one's career journey.

Printing number
10 9 8 7 6 5 4 3 2 1

Dedicated with all my love to my wife, Marta Rodriguez, and our precious daughter, Sofia.

—D. K.

To Angela, who couldn't possibly be more loving and supportive.

—G. W.

CONTENTS

ACKNOWLEDGMENTS

One book written by outside observers can hardly capture every facet of a story that involves millions of people. What we *can* offer, however, is an account of how this movement came to be told through the eyes of some of its participants. This book is based on dozens of interviews with people involved in a grassroots movement. They generously agreed to be interviewed by us, sharing their personal experiences and giving a valuable window into the Market Basket story. Our sincerest thanks to all the members of the extended Market Basket family, with special thanks to the following associates, vendors, customers, government officials, analysts, and others who opened up to us:

Market Basket Associates

Susan Beek, store associate

David Corteau, warehouse associate

Karla Foster, store associate

Dean Joyce, warehouse manager

Linda Kulis, accounts receivable

Mark Lemieux, store director

William Marsden, director of operations

Luis Mendez, warehouse associate

Shawn Moran, store associate

Sean Morse, assistant store director

Barbara Paquette, accounts payable

Scott Patenaude, meat manager

Diane Patterson, refrigeration associate

Steve Paulenka, grocery operations

Joe Schmidt, operations
 supervisor

Tom Trainor, district supervisor
Cindy Whelan, store director

Vendors

Tony and Amal Aboukhater,
 independent contractor
Rich Bonanno, founder,
 Pleasant Valley Gardens
Michael Fairbrother, founder,
 Moonlight Meadery

Jim Fantini, bakery vendor
Tim Malley, chief
 executive officer, Boston
 Sword and Tuna
John Simone, owner,
 Riverside Farm

Customers

Jack Christian
David Greenberg
Linda Heilein

Susan Nolan
Rita Stone
Jaymie Wolfe

Government Officials

State Senator Sal
 DiDomenico, Everett
State Senator Eileen
 Donoghue, Lowell
State Senator Barry
 Finegold, Andover

Governor Maggie Hassan,
 New Hampshire
Rick Sullivan, Chief of
 Staff to Governor Deval
 Patrick, Massachusetts

Analysts

Ted Clark, executive director,
 Northeastern University
 Center for Family Business
Burt Flickinger, managing
 director, Strategic
 Resource Group
Thomas Kochan, professor of
 management, Massachusetts
 Institute of Technology

Miguel Padro, project
 manager, Aspen Institute
James Post, professor of
 management, Boston
 University
Jon Springer, retail editor,
 Supermarket News
Neil Stern, senior partner,
 McMillan Doolittle

Zeynep Ton, associate professor of operations

management, Massachusetts Institute of Technology

Additional Contributors

David Brow, photographer, *Lowell Sun*

Jay Childs, director, JBC Communications

Claire Ignacio, author

Melissa Paly, director of strategy and multimedia, Crosscurrent Communications

Titus Plomaritis, retired chiropractor

William Poulios, family friend

Joanne Sheehan, director, Lowell Council on Aging

Eliot Tatelman, founder, Jordan's Furniture

We wish to single out Jim Fantini for introducing us to associates and other Market Basket stakeholders, for coordinating interviews with senior managers, and for believing in the project from the beginning. His efforts to help us tell the story completely and accurately have greatly enhanced the book.

We also wish to send a special thank you to our colleagues at Drexel University and the *Lowell Sun* for reviewing drafts and providing additional ideas and suggestions. In particular, we thank Anubhav Aggarwal for research support. Thank you also to Maximo Bustillo for his many insightful suggestions, especially in telling the history of the company.

We thank David Brow of the *Lowell Sun* for his beautiful photos. Brow covered the Market Basket story from the beginning and was at the rallies, demonstrations, and other key events.

We also thank the team at AMACOM who have been a pleasure to work with from day one. In particular, we thank Stephen S. Power, who spearheaded this endeavor and helped us craft it into this book. We also thank Tim Durning, who showed great patience and professionalism as we went through versions of the manuscript.

Finally, and above all, we thank our families for their support. Only unconditional love can explain how they tolerated us for the past months. We dominated conversations at dinner with talk of Market Basket, asked them to read excerpts, sought their opinions on what to include in the book, and worked nights, weekends, and holidays to meet our deadlines. Doré, Michael, Suzanne, and Camille Korschun all pored over drafts every step of the way. We hope our loved ones agree that it was worth it!

Thank you.

PROLOGUE

By 9 A.M., thousands had congregated in the parking lot yards away from a Market Basket supermarket. The raucous crowd was a mix of part-time clerks, truck drivers, office workers, store directors, and senior managers from the corporate office. There were teenagers for whom Market Basket is their first employer and longtime employees for whom Market Basket has been their only employer. Also in the crowd were lifelong customers as well as suppliers of produce, fish, and other goods.

It was the third rally in less than a month. The DJ played a parody of Twisted Sister's song "We're Not Gonna Take It" (with the words changed to "We Are Market Basket") over the sound system as cowbells and air horns pierced the air. An airplane circled high above the parking lot, towing a banner that read in red capital letters, "Arthur T. Save Market Basket! Buy Them Out!" Borrowed school buses were arriving regularly now from all over New England—their passengers cheering and waving signs through open windows. Traffic on Boston's Interstate 495 artery was backed up from Stadium Plaza in Tewksbury, Massachusetts, where the rally took place, to Interstate 93, five miles away.

While the rally was boisterous, it was a different story inside Market Basket's stores. Shelves for perishables at the chain's seventy-one stores were barren, most checkouts were closed, and 90 percent or more of the chain's sales (in the neighborhood of $75 million per week) had disappeared. The offices at headquarters were quiet, too. Dozens of office staff had walked out weeks earlier—their cubicles now empty. The regional supermarket powerhouse was, for all intents and purposes, shut down.

Steve Paulenka climbed a few steps to a makeshift podium built on the bed of his pickup truck. Paulenka was perhaps the most visible among a group of former managers leading a rapidly growing movement. Like so many in the crowd, Paulenka was a "lifer" at Market Basket. He was only in his fifties, yet a forty-year veteran of the supermarket chain. Like nearly all supervisors, managers, and executives at Market Basket, he worked his way up the ranks, starting as a teenager bagging groceries and rolling shopping carts in the parking lot. Until a few weeks before this rally, he served as the company's facilities and operations supervisor. As was customary for employees who ranked assistant manager or above, he normally wore a tie. Today, as a *former* Market Basket employee, he wore a baseball cap and golf shirt.

Paulenka was known among colleagues as a man of few words. Like so many at the company, he was not one to seek the limelight. Despite this low-key demeanor, or perhaps because of it, he seemed to have a special talent at the microphone, and he had grown into his role as emcee at these rallies. He looked out over the thousands of Market Basket workers, shoppers, and other supporters and said, "We're blowing the bugle again today, and you have to answer it. I'm sad to have to ask you. You've given so much. But you have to give more . . . we are firm in our resolve. . . . We stay where we are, doing what we're doing, until they return our leader."

That leader is Arthur T. Demoulas, the man who had overseen six years of double-digit growth as Market Basket's CEO and who, over more than forty years with the company, had engendered extraordinary loyalty from his management team, employees, customers, and suppliers. Yet Arthur T.—often referred to as Artie T., or by his initials A. T. D.—was now the former CEO. He had been ousted just weeks before this rally by the company's board of directors. This created a standoff with two opposing sides.

On one side stood the majority shareholders and five of the seven members of the board of directors. This side was led by Arthur T.'s cousin and rival, Arthur S. Demoulas, who used a slim majority stake—50.5 percent—to take control of the board and propose some radical changes. The plan was to shift as much liquidity to the shareholders as possible; this involved leveraging the company—in layman's terms, borrowing money—and paying shareholders an immediate and continuous dividend of all excess cash, starting with $300 million in the fall of 2013. Moreover, the majority shareholders planned to sell their shares, from all appearances, to a Belgian holding company of supermarket brands called Delhaize Group, which owned local competitor Hannaford.

Arthur T. had been the key obstacle to their strategy. So they fired him and replaced him with two new CEOs: Felicia Thornton, who had held executive roles at Albertsons and Kroger, and James "Jim" Gooch, the former CEO of RadioShack with additional executive experience at Sears and Kmart. After taking the reins, the co-CEOs promptly fired eight of Arthur T.'s most faithful managers.

On the other side of this conflict—Arthur T.'s side—were employees (all nonunion workers who call themselves associates), customers, suppliers, and a growing contingent of lawmakers. They were fighting for the man who they believed had always fought for them and whose management style had fostered a unique company culture: He championed profit sharing; bonus checks that often paid four figures or more each year; paid days off if a worker needed to tend to a sick loved one; scholarships to help pay for employees to attend college; low prices, high quality, and exceptional service for customers; and flexibility and reliability to suppliers. His supporters wanted more than to save this man's job, however. They saw this as a struggle to save a culture and business model that was important for New England. Market Basket was more than a grocery store for these people. It represented an ideal. A "way of life" that should not—could not—be tampered with.

Paulenka read what he called "the butcher's bill": a list of those who were fired by the new CEOs or had walked out in solidarity. They now composed a tightly knit management team that represented a growing movement of protesters.

"Joe Garon, forty-nine years,

"Tom Gordon, forty years,

"Tom Trainor, forty-one years . . .

"Jim Miamis—if you count the seven years part time, seventy-six years," he said, pausing for applause, "and one of the finest gentlemen I've ever met."

The list named eighteen senior managers with a combined tenure of more than seven hundred years with the chain.

Then Paulenka turned to the co-CEOs who replaced Arthur T.: "Jim Gooch, three weeks. Felicia Thornton, three weeks." Paulenka paused, allowing the boos to echo among the protesters. "I think that's a bad deal."

—

The stakes were tremendous. Market Basket is a $4.5 billion regional supermarket powerhouse. Unease was setting in about how the region would be affected if the chain reached the point of bankruptcy. If Market Basket were to go under, it could have a ripple effect with devastating consequences.

Jobs would be impacted first. Market Basket directly employs more than twenty-five thousand people. The reduced hours caused by the protest had already been noticed by national agencies; the Bureau of Labor Statistics, in their report the month following the end of the protest, mentioned that an uptick in the U.S. unemployment rate was due in part to events taking place at the supermarket.

Many customers in the region would also suffer. Market Basket has two million customers spanning three states: Massachusetts, New Hampshire, and most recently Maine. Many of these customers belong to vulnerable, low-income populations. With Market Basket as the low-price supermarket in their area, some worried that losing the chain could leave these consumers without a viable alternative for their weekly groceries.

Suppliers, especially local producers of produce and other perishables, relied heavily on Market Basket revenues to meet their own payrolls. Some of these vendors sold only to Market Basket or sold so much to the company that they worried about their own solvency without such a reliable customer.

The conflict showed no signs of abating. Both sides were digging in for a long slog. There was concern among many that the animosity between the two sides was simply too deep to overcome. Recent developments gave little comfort.

Thomas Kochan, a Massachusetts Institute of Technology professor who had followed the dispute all summer, offered a rather sobering assessment. In a column for Boston's National Public Radio affiliate, WBUR, he wrote about his unease: "The tone of this conflict is escalating—and to a potentially dangerous degree. History is littered with the detritus of bitter labor disputes that ended badly . . . To any historian of these events, the fact that the Market Basket dispute's trajectory seems to be heading there is worrisome, to say the least."

John Davis, chair of the Families in Business Program at Harvard University, added, "Not only is the company being drained of money, but its suppliers are being hurt and employees are going without wages. The piling on that happens because of what could really result in this company being destroyed." Sean Willems, an operations professor at Boston University's School of Management, was doubtful that the company could sustain itself through a long protest. "The end game for this has to be sooner [rather] than later," he said on July 29, 2014.

Industry analysts largely came to the same conclusions. "The company's cash position is lousy," said Kevin Griffin, publisher of the *Griffin Report of Food Marketing*. "It's in a really tough spot right now." Jeff Menzer, publisher of the *Food Trade News*, also observed that "whatever cash reserve they have is being frittered away." He suggested that Market Basket's leadership needed to take action or face bankruptcy.

Governor Maggie Hassan of New Hampshire knew early on that failure to reach some form of agreement would impact her state. Governor Deval Patrick of Massachusetts was initially reluctant to enter the fray but eventually was forced to join Governor Hassan in a supporting role. In a letter to the board of directors (directed at both sides of the dispute), he took a scolding tone, which underscored the dangers: "By any measure, the disruption that followed your recent change in CEO has gotten out of hand," Patrick said. "Your failure to resolve this matter is not only hurting the company's brand and business, but also many innocent and relatively powerless workers whose livelihoods depend on you."

How did it come to this? Nearly all family businesses have stories of internal rivalries and behind-the-scene intrigue. This was different. This went well beyond the quarrels and grudges found at other companies. It was a family dispute so formidable that it cast a dark cloud over the region.

—

Unprecedented. That is the word so often used to describe the Market Basket protests. Never before had nonunion employees banded together to reinstate a fired CEO. Never before had a protest involved such a broad coalition of employees: from cashiers to store directors to truck drivers to office workers, and all levels of management. Never before had a worker protest spilled over, involving both customers and suppliers, all working in unison to shut down a company this large for this long.

This is the story of one of New England's most admired companies reaching the brink of collapse. It is the story of a battle over the future of a company—a battle that pitted cousin against cousin, employees and customers against shareholders, and some say good against evil.

The Market Basket story is the result of a combination of events that occurred over nearly a century. The history of the Demoulas family, the management style that Arthur T. developed, and the unique culture seen at every level of the company all created a potent mix that not only ignited the protests but also enabled a grassroots movement to spread and ultimately become successful.

In the pages that follow, we trace the protests all the way back to the origins of the company nearly one hundred years ago. We argue that from that history emerged the unique culture at Market Basket. It is a culture based on service to the community, a sense of family, empowerment, and a willingness to break with convention. That culture is embraced by associates from Arthur T. and his upper-level executive team all the way to frontline employees—it became the foundation on which a successful company and an unlikely protest was built. The protest was marked by a deep sense of purpose that saving Market Basket would save New England; a loyalty to the Market Basket family that created fierce commitment among associates, customers, and vendors; a commitment to excellence that produced great discipline; and a belief in experience over textbook theory that resulted in a willingness to throw away the rulebook set forth by the board, scholars, or the media.

Market Basket is unique. It is tempting to think that because the story of the protest is unprecedented, it can't be replicated. In fact, the Market Basket story holds lessons for managers, for employees, for customers, and for owners. Managers will find unconventional yet effective ways to motivate their workforce. Individuals will find an inspirational story that reveals the hidden power they wield. Above all, the story forces us to rethink who really owns a company and who gets to decide how it is run.

PART ONE

Imagine you walk into the supermarket at 170 Everett Avenue in Chelsea, Massachusetts. It's the flagship of one of New England's largest supermarket chains. As you approach the sliding glass doors, you can already hear the rattles of shopping carriages and the crinkling of shopping bags inside. Aside from the larger-than-normal crowd, the supermarket appears typical enough.

But then, as you enter, you begin to notice subtle differences. The store is a bit of a throwback to another era. White and salmon-colored tiles adorn the floors in a quasi-checkerboard motif, giving the store somewhat of a 1950s feel. There are no frills. Displays are simple, with more emphasis on information than production value.

All the male employees (they call themselves *associates*) dress in white shirts and ties. Store managers wear red jackets, and clerks and others wear blue. Each associate wears a tag with his or her name and the number of years he or she has been at Market Basket. Some associates who look to be in their midthirties have nametags that say "20 years." It would mean that they started at fourteen or fifteen years of age. They probably did.

The floor is crowded with people—families, young and old. The ethnic background is diverse, and odds are good you will hear a mother speaking Spanish (or another language) to a child.

As you walk down the aisle, you weave your way past boxes of newly shipped products being unloaded by other associates. Market Basket does most of its stocking during the day while customers are shopping. This has the happy side effect of placing an employee in nearly every aisle; if you have trouble finding something, there is probably an employee within eyeshot.

The prices are low—extremely low. By all accounts, Market Basket manages to beat the prices of competitors item for item. Just prior to the protest, New Hampshire Public Radio visited Market Basket and its main competitors, Shaw's and Hannaford, and bought the same twelve items (same brand and size) across multiple departments. The exact same basket of goods cost $48.74 at Shaw's, $40.60 at Hannaford, and only $35.85 at Market Basket. A half gallon of Breyer's ice cream, to cite one example, cost nearly double at Shaw's compared with Market Basket.

When it's time to check out, you notice that nearly every register is open. Each register has a two-person team; typically, it consists of a clean-cut young man bagging groceries and a young woman at the cash register. You do not see any of the automated self-checkout machines that are in fashion at other chains. As Chief Executive Officer Arthur T. Demoulas likes to say, it's simply "a person serving another person."

This is Market Basket.

At the time of writing, the chain has seventy-five stores in three states: Massachusetts, New Hampshire, and Maine. More than two million New Englanders shop there each week. It's a $4.5 billion supermarket chain that retains its mom-and-pop feel. Market Basket is a family-owned business, and it has been since its inception almost one hundred years ago.

The company does none of the branding that Shaw's and other grocers spend millions on. Yet Market Basket was shown in customer surveys to be among the best nationally. A customer rating survey published in 2012 by *Consumer Reports* ranked Market Basket seventh in the country among more than fifty of the top grocers, based on service, perishables, price, and cleanliness. It was rated best on price and was given a score of eighty-two out of a possible one hundred points.

Market Basket's unique way of doing things evolved over almost a century. The culture we see at Market Basket today began to take shape early in the twentieth century when two Greek immigrants committed to serving their low-income and working-class neighbors opened a small storefront in Lowell, Massachusetts.

1

"You've Never Met a Family Like This"

It is hard to imagine a more challenging time and place to open a grocery than 1917 in Lowell. But that's when Market Basket got its start in this mill city on the Merrimack River about twenty-five miles north of Boston. In the late 1800s, Lowell had been heralded as a beacon of the Northeast. The first two decades of the twentieth century were a different story. Lowell's fortunes were on a downturn.

The city had previously relied on the Merrimack River to generate endless, relatively low-cost hydropower. This enabled decades of growth, turning the Merrimack Valley into a stalwart of the textile industry. But the rise of coal as a cheap alternative energy source turned Lowell's competitive advantage into a competitive shortcoming. Its infrastructure was inflexible, and the mills began to close one by one. Textile companies moved their mills to seaport locations, which could receive coal shipments more cheaply.

As jobs dried up, unease hung heavy in the region. The unease fueled a number of worker strikes at mills in the region, the most famous of which is the Bread and Roses Strike in nearby Lawrence, Massachusetts. During that strike, about thirty thousand textile workers walked off their jobs for two-and-a-half months during a bitter winter in 1912. The struggle began on New Year's Day, when legislation took effect reducing the workweek from fifty-six to fifty-four hours. The law was supposed to provide relief for workers, but companies responded by reducing overall weekly pay. A group of workers at the Everett Mill opened their paychecks to find a pay reduction of $0.32 (the average weekly pay for these workers was $8.76). The cut translated into roughly four loaves of bread per week for families of mill employees. They walked off the job and demonstrated, chanting, "Short pay! Short pay!"

The Industrial Workers of the World (known as the Wobblies) appealed to a wide range of workers affected by the pay cut. Mostly the workers were immigrants from southern and eastern European countries, as well as parts of the Middle East. They were separated by cultural, religious, and linguistic differences. Determined not to let those differences interfere with their resolve, the Wobblies recruited representatives from English, Polish, Greek, Italian, and other backgrounds. The protesters became bound by a common need to improve their living and working conditions.

A walkout at the Everett Mill quickly spread to others in Lawrence as more and more disgruntled workers joined in. Within a week, their numbers had swelled to ten thousand. Their demands were straightforward: a 15 percent increase in wages, double pay for overtime work, and a pledge from owners to not retaliate against strikers.

A majority of the workers in the mills of Lawrence were women and children, and the protest gained strength from the feminist movement of that time. They were fiercely determined to change the way ownership was operating the mills, showing "lots of cunning and also lots of bad temper," according to one mill boss. One group of women cornered a police officer, stripped him of his uniform, and tossed him over a bridge into the icy waters below. Such civil disobedience led the district attorney, Harry Atwell, to comment that "one policeman can handle 10 men, while it takes 10 policemen to handle one woman."

The strikers dug in for a long struggle; they formed relief committees that provided food, medical care, and clothing to families left without an income. The companies hired thugs to intimidate the protesters. The governor of Massachusetts sent state police and militia to fire-hose picketers. This only enflamed tempers more. Their resolve and unity remained intact. One magazine observed, "At first everyone predicted that it would be impossible to mold these divergent people together, but aside from the skilled men, comparatively few [broke the strike and] went back to the mills."

Workers continued picketing and clashed violently with authorities over weeks, destroying machinery at the mills. At protest parades, demonstrators carried banners demanding not only a living wage but also a more dignified workplace. "We want bread, and roses, too," they chanted, drawing from a populist poem by James Oppenheim called "Bread and Roses."

After weeks of struggle, the American Woolen Company finally agreed to all the strikers' demands on March 12, 1912. Within a few weeks, most other mills had too. Before long, factories across New England also raised pay and shortened the workweek in fear of similar repercussions. The strike is now remembered as among the first in which workers from multiple ethnicities united to improve their working conditions; it was a protest where they demanded dignity in the workplace and won.

—

Against this backdrop of economic challenge and labor strife, a young man arrived in Lowell. His name was Athanasios Demoulas. In Greek, *athanasios* means "immortal." Demoulas, which shares the root "demo" in democracy, carries connotations of one who serves the public welfare.

Athanasios, or Arthur, as he later became known, departed from his native Greece in order to avoid the strife that had already taken his father's life. He was twenty-three when he landed at Ellis Island on St. Patrick's Day in 1906. Rumor has it that his hopes were so grandiose that as he walked the streets of New York City to catch the train to Lowell, he mused that the holiday parade was for him.

His entrance may have felt grand to him, but his story was common for that time. There would be thousands of other immigrants with similar dreams, facing similar obstacles. Throughout the 1800s, the success of Lowell's textile mills drew a steady stream of workers. According to the Lowell Historical Society, more than a third of all Lowell residents at that time were foreign born. They first arrived from Quebec—Lowell was sometimes referred to as Little Canada because of the influx of French Canadians. Subsequent waves of immigrants came from Europe, with a spike in Greek arrivals around the early twentieth century. Athanasios Demoulas arrived toward the end of that Greek wave.

By the time Demoulas arrived, the mark of Greeks in Lowell was already indelible. Greek Orthodox churches had sprung up, Greek coffeehouses had started to appear, and construction had begun on the Greek Holy Trinity Church. Organizations such as the Washington-Acropolis Society formed to advance the fortunes of Greek immigrants. Despite their growing influence in the region, life remained challenging. Greek employees had gained a reputation not only for their hard work but also for being challenging to manage. For a time, Bigelow Carpet Company and others refused to hire people of Greek origin because of a series of strikes thought to be organized by the Hellenic community.

Athanasios settled in the Acre, a section of Lowell nestled near an elbow of the Merrimack River that was being populated by a rapidly growing Greek community. (It is still known by many as "Greektown.") Once he settled in, he sent for his fiancée, Efrosine Soulis, who was waiting for him in his home village of Meteora. They married in 1914. Demoulas first found work in a tannery as a shoemaker. But before long, the poor working conditions in the factory began to affect his health. A doctor advised him to find new work away from the factory setting.

So Athanasios and Efrosine opened a modest grocery—one of a dozen in the neighborhood. Perhaps to give it an air of sophistication, they capitalized the "M" in Demoulas, calling it DeMoulas Market. The shop was located on Dummer Street on the western edge of downtown Lowell. It was frequented by mostly poor and working-class members of the Greek community who picked up meats and other foods on their way to the mills. He also delivered groceries free of charge. In those days, it was common for customers to buy on credit. Especially in immigrant cities, customers would run a tab during the week and then pay the balance on payday. A great number of Demoulas's customers paid this way, making him part grocer, part banker, all the while keeping him closely tied to the fortunes of Lowell's working poor.

The Demoulases worked hard—very hard. Their store was only six hundred square feet, but they were ambitious and hoped to make a name for themselves for their fresh lamb. Workers on their way to the mills began to stop by the store for one of Efrosine's roasted pork sandwiches, a specialty for which she was gaining a reputation. The couple did their own slaughtering. To keep up with growing demand, Athanasios had to make multiple trips per week to the railroad yards to pick up live pigs and sheep. After a few years, they bought land in the adjacent town of Dracut, where they developed a farm to raise cows, pigs, goats, chickens, and ducks.

By outward appearances, the Demoulases were an average, hard-working family, reaching for the American dream. But as Richard Fichera, a thirty-three-year Market Basket associate from Danville, New Hampshire, put it at one of the demonstrations in 2013, "You've never met a family like this."[1]

—

Athanasios and Efrosine had six children, four of whom survived past childhood. The oldest was John, born in 1915. Two years after opening DeMoulas Market, they had George. Their third son was born in 1920, and they named him after the son of Odysseus, Telemachus. Roughly translated, his name means "far fighter," foreshadowing the many years of court battles he would one day endure. Ann was born two years later in 1922. They lost a baby girl in 1919 and then Evangelos at the age of five in 1930.

---

1. Several quotations in this book are from conversations with the authors at rallies and other demonstrations in 2013 and 2014. They will not be cited individually forthwith.

The Great Depression of the 1930s hit doubly hard in the Lowell area, a city already reeling from closing mills and subsequent unemployment. While sales were slow, Athanasios did what he could to help those even less fortunate. He would give poor customers groceries on credit or a free piece of bread with ham. These gestures of kindness left a mark on his sons, especially his son Telemachus, who was already enamored of the grocery business.

Their sense of charity didn't help their cause, however, and in 1938, they faced foreclosure themselves. Cash was tight, as many of the customers who bought on credit had trouble following through on their bills. The bank demanded a $100 payment—about $1,700 in today's dollars. With their cash flow dwindling, this represented the greatest threat to the Demoulas's store since opening twenty years earlier. Athanasios assured his son that he and Efrosine would find a way to reimburse the bank. But the situation was so dire that Telemachus, who also went by Mike, insisted on dropping out of school to help keep the market afloat. They found a way to raise the funds and saved their business.

But the scar of that traumatic experience remained. Remembering how close they had come to losing everything, Telemachus never relaxed for a moment. During World War II, Telemachus's older brother George served in the army. Stationed in Guadalcanal, he joked in his letters home about Telemachus's work ethic: "Please remind him when the day is over because he is liable to work through one of these moonlit nights figuring that it is still daytime."

After the war, George returned, but his immediate plans were not to join the family business; he had dreams of starting a trucking company. However, Telemachus wanted George to join him at the market so that he could expand the business. He saw opportunity beyond the Acre but knew he couldn't do it alone. In the end, George became convinced that joining forces in the market held the most promise for the whole family. He eventually became the business's executive vice president and treasurer.

By 1950, Telemachus and George had found enough success to expand the original store, doubling it in size. Two years later, they made it official. They bought the business from their parents for $15 thousand. Another expansion in 1956 would send sales soaring, and soon the brothers knew they were onto something.

Now that they had honed a winning formula, which combined a wide selection with quality goods and good service, the next phase would be to open additional stores. The Demoulas brothers opened a second store on nearby Bridge Street in the Centralville neighborhood of Lowell, a residential area just across the Merrimack River. It was also a dream come true for Athanasios and Efrosine, who had always wanted the business to stay in the family. Athanasios was there to cut the ribbon at the opening. It was to be his only store opening. The family patriarch died six months later at age seventy-five.

Their father had left a legacy of serving the working families of Lowell by providing high-quality goods with exceptional service. These are the same components of the Market Basket formula we see today. Telemachus and George used these components, together with uncommon tenacity and drive, to build one of the most admired supermarkets in the country.

Everything was in place to catch the supermarket revolution.

2

"They Caught the Supermarket Revolution"

In the early twentieth century, shopping was, to say the least, inconvenient. It was not uncommon for a household to purchase dairy, meats, and produce from three different stores. Each of the specialty stores was heavy on service, with most of the food behind the counter.

But in the 1940s and 1950s, a new type of grocery operation emerged: the supermarket. Industry analysts today classify supermarkets mainly by the number of stock-keeping units (SKUs) they carry; each SKU refers to a different variety of a product. For example, each brand of toothpaste has a variety of flavors or package sizes, each with its own SKU code. Supermarkets carry anywhere between fifteen and sixty thousand SKUs. To put this in perspective, Trader Joe's carries between four and five thousand SKUs, while a superstore such as Walmart or BJ's Wholesale Club might carry on the order of seventy to one hundred thousand SKUs.

Telemachus Demoulas, one of the two brothers who had taken over their parents' grocery store, noticed the trend toward more SKUs and, more than anyone else in the family, saw a tremendous opportunity. The new format required a much larger space than the six hundred square feet they had at the time, but he figured that if they sold enough volume to cover overhead, the model could be extremely profitable. If they could be a leader in this trend, the Demoulas family might even be able to open multiple supermarkets.

The supermarket innovation put a full line of groceries, including meat, produce, deli, and bakery items, under the same roof. And while shopkeepers would collect fruit and other goods for customers from behind a counter in smaller stores, supermarkets brought a new form of self-service to grocery shopping by using the familiar warehouse style we know today: customers pick their own items from the shelves and then check them out at a dedicated cash register.

The new format was a learning experience for eighteen-year-old Claire Ignacio, who took a job as their first cashier. She had to attend cash register school. "This was a whole new thing, a register," said Ignacio, who, at eighty-three, still works a few days a week behind a desk at a chiropractor's office. "The cash registers didn't tell you how to give change in those days. You had to do it yourself." But it was an exciting time. We take it for granted today, but she was a part of something new. "It was the first big market in the area," she said. "A *super* market."

Even under the new format, the Demoulas brothers maintained ties to the old way of doing things. They continued the practice of selling on credit; customers kept a tab. Another quirk that endured into the supermarket era was the brothers' sale of live chickens. "The Greek people, they didn't want a dead chicken. They wanted to kill it themselves," Ignacio said.

There was at first some apprehension about Telemachus and George's new cashier. Ignacio was of French background, and it wasn't clear yet whether she would click with their overwhelmingly Greek clientele. She had to prove herself, but her bosses created a welcoming atmosphere that she grew to love. Telemachus, she said, was "stern and bossy" but "very kindhearted." George, she said, "was a barrel full of laughs." He taught Ignacio a few key Greek phrases, including "Happy Easter."

Once she demonstrated her loyalty to Telemachus and George and their business, she said, she "won them over." She maintains a special fondness for George, who used to tease her constantly. "George and I were like this," she said, interlocking her index and middle fingers. "They were special," she said of the brothers.

Ignacio stopped working at Demoulas when she became pregnant at age twenty, but she continued to follow the company. Like many former employees today, there is an appreciation, almost a nostalgia, that remains. She had not seen either brother for more than two decades when she bumped into Telemachus at the Market Basket on Bridge Street in Lowell in 1978. As executives are known to do today at the company, Telemachus recognized her immediately and gave her a warm welcome. She told him how shocked she was that he would remember her after all these years. "How could I ever forget my first cashier?" was his response.

—

A young man who delivered chickens to the supermarket was Titus Plomaritis. Now an eighty-five-year-old retired chiropractor who lives in nearby Pelham, New Hampshire, Plomaritis would, from the age of twelve, help skin and prepare the chickens each Friday at the family farm on Johnson Street in Lowell. On Saturdays, he would carry double-lined plastic bags in each hand, taking the bus from Varnum Avenue in the then-quiet Pawtucketville neighborhood across the Merrimack River and into downtown Lowell.

Each chicken was for someone who had reserved it the week before. Plomaritis would get off the bus at City Hall and then walk the short distance down Dummer Street where he would meet Telemachus about halfway to the store. Telemachus would dump the chickens onto a weight scale, writing down their weight on a piece of paper that Plomaritis would give to his father. His father, a Greek immigrant who never learned to speak English, would walk down to the store from the nearby barber shop he owned to collect his payment each Monday.

Plomaritis built a close friendship with Telemachus despite being much younger in age. When Plomaritis became a star running back for the legendary late 1940s Lowell High School football team, Telemachus and Jim Miamis would often attend, he said. And he kept such a close relationship with Telemachus over the years that Plomaritis even wrote a chapter about their friendship in a 539-page autobiography published in 2012.

"He was like a big brother," Plomaritis said. "He was so kind."

To this day, Plomaritis shops only at Market Basket. When Telemachus still worked there, he said, "Every time I'd go into the store, he'd put his arm around me."

Plomaritis had a chance encounter with Telemachus on the shores of Palm Beach in 1975 when Plomaritis was in town taking the Florida state chiropractic exam. Telemachus was there on vacation with his daughter.

The two men never missed a beat, recalling their old days on Dummer Street and Plomaritis's football games. "You carried that football much faster than you carried those two bags of chickens," Plomaritis remembered Telemachus telling him that day.

A few decades later, when Plomaritis began compiling memories for his autobiography, he thought back to that unlikely meeting in Palm Beach. He knew Telemachus had two daughters but couldn't remember which was at the beach that day. So Plomaritis called the only Demoulas name he could find in the phone book: Telemachus's son, Arthur T.

Not only did Arthur T. return Plomaritis's call, but he gave him a tour of the massive Tewksbury warehouse and arranged for him to meet Glorianne, Arthur's sister and Telemachus's daughter, who was in Palm Beach that day. Telemachus and Arthur T. were certainly father and son, he told himself after that day.

"I would never shop anywhere else," Plomaritis said. Of Arthur T., he added, "He's aces, I'll tell you. There's no one better."

—

Telemachus and George kept expanding, opening one new store a year for fourteen years. Professor Jim Post of Boston University says, "The two brothers, [Telemachus] and George, they expanded the business, and they caught the supermarket revolution so that when the small stores disappeared, they made the move to the supermarket model and established Market Basket as a supermarket chain."

It's difficult to imagine today just how bold this idea was. The idea of creating a chain would have been preposterous to most people in the neighborhood. But as cars became more common, even among the working class, supermarkets became a practical way for families to shop. They shopped less frequently, often weekly, but were able to fill the car with groceries. In other parts of the country, A&P and Kroger were pouncing on this trend and expanding rapidly.

The public housing projects that still define the parameters of the Acre would be built after the war, and Telemachus and George capitalized on the needs of growing families there. They opened a new store to replace the original in 1950 and then, after buying the business from their parents, expanded it in 1956. In those six years, annual sales went from $2 thousand to $900 thousand.

The Demoulas family had an additional advantage, and that was their long history in the neighborhood. Other families that owned grocery stores in the Acre had sons, but only the Demoulas boys took over their parents' store, and only their market survived. Success, Telemachus said, came from continuity. Continuity came from the strong relationships they had forged over several decades.

They also used their neighborhood ties to find skilled managers. George, by all accounts the more gregarious one, brought in friends he knew from the Greek social circuit. For example, George was president of the Holy Trinity Greek Orthodox Church in Lowell and met friends who became employees or did contract work: accounting, banking, and buying for the stores. Many had ties to the Demoulas family since they were boys in the Acre.

—

One man who saw the expansion from beginning to end was William Poulios. Poulios grew up in Lowell and has known the Demoulas family since he was a small child. He now lives in the neighboring town of Chelmsford on the circle at the end of a cul-de-sac. Poulios fought in the Battle of the Bulge and, for his courage, received the *Legion d'Honneur*, one of the most distinguished awards in France. Now at ninety-two years old, he has a large family that lives in Massachusetts and New Hampshire. Family members can be seen milling around the house, along with a nurse or two, tending to Poulios and his wife. His deep-blue eyes suggest a long memory, and he is full of stories of the Demoulas family. His father shopped at the original DeMoulas Market, and now his great grandchildren are loyal shoppers.

Known to friends as Bill or Willy, Poulios is no stranger to the interview. The Market Basket saga has brought more journalists to his home than his family would like to count. Perhaps it is this experience with interviewers that enables him to immediately launch into anecdotes of the Demoulas family from decades ago. He begins the first story so quickly, it is as if he were completing an unfinished sentence from a previous interview.

He darts through time, recounting stories of grandfather Athanasios, Telemachus, George, John, Arthur T., Arthur S., and others in the family. A story from one decade flows into another or is interrupted altogether when a new thought triggers an anecdote that Poulios feels is more telling than the last. Trying to put the stories in context as one listens is a fascinating yet almost dizzying experience.

When asked about this friendship with the Demoulas family, he says that his bonds run deeper than friendship; he always felt he was a part of the extended family. Poulios remembers holding both Arthur T. and Arthur S. at their christenings. Whenever his family was in need, the Demoulas family was there, giving a loan or a favor as the situation required.

Poulios is well aware of the rift in the family between Telemachus's descendants and George's. While Poulios respects the larger family, his fondest memories are clearly of Telemachus's—Arthur T.'s— side of the family, for whom he is an unabashed supporter. He and Telemachus used to have breakfast together most Saturdays for many years. His loyalty to Telemachus was shared by his father, who he says "wouldn't have anyone else but [Telemachus] cut his meat, the way he liked his lamb."

His earliest memories of Telemachus were as a young child. Poulios remembers, probably around the age of ten or eleven, trying to sneak an orange from the shelf at DeMoulas Market. Telemachus, at this point still a child himself, scolded Poulios for his sticky fingers. Then Athanasios stepped in to spoil Poulios as a grandparent might: "Let Bill have a taste, Telemachus." Listening to the story, it's easy to think that Poulios was a Demoulas child.

Poulios was the president of his church, a church that benefited many times from Telemachus's generosity. Poulios once asked him for some help painting it. Telemachus inquired further. He wanted the job to be done completely. In the end, he saw that Poulios not only had the painting done but also added carpeting, restored the icons, and provided the *epitafios*, the embroidered cloth that represents the body of Jesus in Greek churches. Then, as if to demonstrate that his friend wasn't getting special treatment, he brought Poulios into his office and showed him a list of more than one hundred churches he had helped in similar ways.

This kindness extended to his employees as well. One employee approached Telemachus while Poulios was visiting him in his office. The employee asked for a couple of days off work to take care of his daughter who was just diagnosed with cancer; surgery was scheduled in a Boston hospital. With no hesitation, Telemachus told him to take all the time he needed. Then, without being asked, Poulios said, "He pulled his desktop open, made out a check, gave it to him and said, 'you need any more, let me know.'" He told Poulios on many occasions that unless he took good care of his employees, the business couldn't function effectively.

According to Poulios, the Demoulas sense of loyalty goes back to their Greek upbringing: "If you're family, they are going to take care of you. If you're down, they are going to help you. They're gonna feed you at holidays. If you work for them, they are going to invite you to their home. It's the old way of doing things. They brought the old customs back here. It's love and respect first." Poulios was there in the days that Telemachus and George discussed whether they should expand beyond their two stores. George initially resisted the idea, and the brothers were at a stalemate. Telemachus briefly considered going it alone, but fortunately, George came to realize that it was the right move for them.

Although he mostly disagrees with Arthur S.'s version of events, he refuses to enter the family feud. Instead, he downplays the disagreements and describes, matter-of-factly, how the desires of the family diverged, with Telemachus's side of the family maintaining a passion for the grocery business and George's side becoming disinterested and drawn to other interests.

—

Relatives corroborate Poulios's stories. They recall how Telemachus Demoulas still loved to roll up his sleeves and fix a grocery display or show a new assistant produce manager the ropes. "My father didn't have a lot of pastimes; he wasn't a tennis player or a golf player," his son Arthur T. once told the *Boston Globe*, "What he had was his work and his family. He had a great ear for the customer and a lot of respect for their hard-earned money. He saw value in a good, clean, well-operated store where a housewife would be told hello when she came in and thank you when she went out. He was a merchant's merchant."

Telemachus was also a pillar of the community. Having learned charity from his father, Telemachus gave millions of dollars to causes ranging from programs for the blind to college scholarships. He became one of the region's foremost philanthropists. He is also credited with helping to revitalize his old neighborhood by building a new supermarket in the area and pouring his own money into improving the infrastructure. "It was a substantial investment that in any other community would be paid for by the city," Robert Kennedy, the administrator of the Lowell Regional Transit Authority, told the *Associated Press*. "Looking back over the years, his contributions were endless."

—

Demoulas Super Markets was owned by Telemachus and his wife, Irene, and George and his wife, Evanthea. The couples had equal shares. Telemachus and George became the closest of friends and their families the closest of families. Both men married Greek American women and had four children in rapid succession.

Over the years, the men would remain close, godfathers to one another's children. Both named a son Arthur, honoring their father by adapting his name to the language of their adopted homeland. People joked that the only way the brothers failed in symmetry was in something they couldn't control: George and Evanthea had two girls and two boys; Telemachus and Irene had three girls and a boy, Arthur T. Demoulas. Their children played together on the streets of Lowell, Dracut, and later Andover.

In 1964, knowing heart disease ran in their family, they each wrote up a will, signed by the other brother, making each the executor of the other's estate and committing to assuming responsibility for the other's family upon that brother's death.

Then, in 1971, tragedy struck. George was vacationing with his family in Greece on June 27 when his wife woke up that Sunday morning to find him dead of a heart attack in their hotel room. At fifty-one, he had seemed in perfect health. Only the night before, he and his younger son had left the rest of the family after dinner to listen to Greek music at an Athens rooftop bar.

Telemachus stood next to Evanthea for ten hours at his brother's wake, and each day for months following that, he would visit his relatives daily to check on them. He treated George's four children as his own and gave them jobs in the ever-growing chain.

After the passing of his brother, partner, and best friend, Telemachus forged on with the business. A relative would later recall that George's death left a "vacuum in the family hierarchy." That vacuum invited jealousy and conflict. It eventually led to accusations and a series of high-profile lawsuits. Nevertheless, the next thirty years brought continued expansion, continuing the impressive pace of more than one store opening per year.

—

Burt Flickinger tells of some of the open secrets behind the success of Market Basket during this period of expansion. Flickinger is the managing director at Strategic Resource Group, a leading consumer industry business consulting firm headquartered in New York City. He is a fountain of knowledge on the supermarket industry.

Flickinger credits the successful expansion of the business to Telemachus and George's ability to serve families living on fixed and limited incomes. Three generations of families had been economically stranded since the textile mills moved away from the region in the early twentieth century. Flickinger says that one of Demoulas's salient strengths is that the chain "raises consumers' standard of living through low prices."

In the 1960s, large supermarket chains were beginning to charge slotting fees to suppliers. When Unilever or any other supplier wants to sell an item in a supermarket, it generally pays a fee. This is the "cost of entry" to get on the shelf in many chains, and it can range from $10 thousand to more than $250 thousand for a cluster of a dozen or so stores. The slotting fees shift risk to the supplier and are highly profitable for supermarkets.

George Demoulas recognized early on, according to Flickinger, that Stop & Shop, Shaw's, and others were charging hefty slotting fees. He also knew that New England was rich with food manufacturers and farms. Many of these were relatively small and were being shut out by the slotting fee procedure. George turned to small, local operations like Ken's Salad Dressing, which grew out of Ken's steakhouse in Saugus, Massachusetts. Ken's offered a terrific-tasting product, but at the time, it was still selling out of the trunk of a car and had only succeeded in very small, independent stores. While other chains turned Ken's away with exorbitant slotting fees, Demoulas gave it a chance. Ken's is now one of the largest salad dressing brands in the country.

Cape Cod Potato Chips was another beneficiary of the Demoulases' openness to local producers. Like Ken's, it offered a high-quality product but did not have deep enough pockets to break into other chains. Market Basket took Cape Cod early on, helping it grow into a nationally recognized brand.

Ken's and Cape Cod obviously benefited from the deals, but so did Market Basket. These upstart brands helped Market Basket gain a reputation for having an unusual selection of high-quality products at very low prices. Rather than pay premium prices for national brands at the big chains, customers could find great deals on upstart brands. This is what Flickinger means when he says that Market Basket improves low-income people's standard of living.

Another deliberate move that benefited Market Basket customers was maintaining their high-quality meats. Since the 1980s, many chains have shifted to "case-ready" or government-grade meats, in which around 10 percent of the meat's weight is saline (more or less salt water). Market Basket bucked this trend and stuck to "choice" and other high-quality meats. Market Basket is able to sustain this practice today because it has such high volumes per store. Local suppliers are giving Market Basket lower-truckload prices, lower even than Shaw's, Walmart, and other major chains. Meanwhile, even stores like Trader Joe's have moved to case-ready meats.

Another key to Market Basket's growth was the placement of its stores. While other chains sought to expand as widely as possible, as quickly as possible, Market Basket often preferred to saturate a city. Telemachus was perfectly happy being the only player with two or three stores in a single low-income area. This reduced competition and concentrated promotional costs on a smaller area.

The higher store density in low-income areas also paid off big when the northwest section of the 128 Corridor (the suburban area of Boston that follows the Route 128 highway) began to reawaken during the tech boom of the 1990s. Market Basket suddenly found itself a dominant player in some fast-growing districts. Moreover, Market Basket owned a lot of the real estate it operated on, and in some of these areas had paid rock-bottom prices for the land. The combination of high productivity per property and low overhead led to fantastic profits.

But the biggest success factor, according to Flickinger, is their commitment to fully staffed and fully stocked stores. Competitors continue to rely on quick-fix solutions to reduce costs. This usually means cutting staff and reducing the hours of those who remain. They then cut the inventory levels. It's a double whammy on store productivity because the workforce can become demoralized, and customers become frustrated when they can't get help or find the products they need. Supercenter stores might only have four to eight checkout lanes open, even during peak hours. To add insult to injury, chains like Walmart have discontinued profit-sharing plans, which further distances employees from company goals.

Market Basket has a wholly different philosophy. Flickinger explains, "Market Basket looks at store staffing and service as an investment, where all their competitors look at store labor as being an expense." That means that even when the store is at its most crowded, customers know they will be taken care of quickly. All the checkouts will be open, the deli line will move fast, and the produce will be refilled immediately.

To get a sense of how strong the Market Basket model is, Flickinger cites the recent case of Stop & Shop. Stop & Shop acquired Purity Supreme and A&P, giving it a stranglehold on Cape Cod. But the stranglehold was loosened when Market Basket recently opened a store in Bourne, just over one of two bridges that lead to the Cape. The new location became an immediate sensation. It pulled in around three million dollars in revenue per week in the opening month, outpacing many of its established stores and far exceeding the average American supermarket. Customers raved, and they flocked from miles around.

But Market Basket executives have made some mistakes too. Beginning with Telemachus and George, there has always been an "insistence in self-developing all the supermarkets," says Flickinger. Owning the land that the supermarket sits on has benefits for financing of course, but he says, "Strategically, they had a blind spot in terms of competitive entry." When competitors like Bradlees, Caldor, and others went bankrupt over the past few decades, Market Basket passed up opportunities to claim their spaces. Had they been more aggressive in seizing storefront space, they might have been able to stem the influx of entrants, including Target and Walmart. This has made the current environment perhaps more challenging than it had to be. Still, Market Basket was and is a highly successful venture by just about any standard.

—

The most trying time during the Telemachus years was the 1990s, when a dispute over who owned how much of the business threatened the company for the first time. It marred what otherwise was a period of extraordinary growth. It was a phase in which the Demoulas family was dragged through one court battle after another.

Telemachus and George had always differed in opinion on how quickly to expand their chain. After George died, Telemachus set out on a path of rapid expansion that brought the company down much of the road to where it is now, from fourteen stores to fifty-eight. As he led this expansion, he established trust funds for George's four children, giving each $25 thousand a year until age thirty. Additionally, each month, he deposited $10 thousand into his sister-in-law's checking account and gave each of her children stipends: a few hundred dollars per month when they were younger, then $5 thousand per month when they were adults. (Adjusted to today's dollars, it would be equivalent to more than $250 thousand per year.) They also owned shares in the business, which paid dividends. They took trips to the Mediterranean and Caribbean, and Telemachus would pay for a lavish lifestyle for his nieces and nephews. George's oldest son, Evan, raced Formula I cars in Europe and amassed a collection of Corvettes, Porsches, and BMWs. Arthur S., who still worked as an assistant produce director for the company, had a collection of Ferraris. Telemachus bought two apartments for Arthur S.'s sister, Fotene, in Boston's

Back Bay neighborhood, paying $631 thousand in cash. And when Fotene wanted to open an art gallery, Telemachus set her up with a team of lawyers and accountants.

Most new stores during that later expansion were incorporated under a different company name, Market Basket. Telemachus always asserted that a separate company was necessary because liquor license laws limited sales per company in New Hampshire. With two separate companies, twice as many licenses were available. In contrast, Arthur S.'s side of the family claimed that the primary goal of the changes was not to conform to liquor laws but to reduce their stake in the company. They essentially charged Telemachus with stealing their equity. An attorney for Telemachus's side, however, painted George's heirs as acquisitive: "Being millionaires isn't good enough," he said. "They want to be multi-, multi-, multi-millionaires."

The differences grew into an argument, which grew into a lawsuit, which grew into a media circus. It was a family dispute played out on a public stage with hundreds of millions of dollars at stake. The central lawsuit was, in dollar terms, one of the biggest decisions in Massachusetts's history. "The venomous case has overtones of both soap opera and tragedy, all rooted in the rise of a Greek-American family, from humble origins to one of the region's wealthiest and most successful," the *Boston Globe* reported. It was referred to somewhat tongue-in-cheek as a Greek tragedy. Another article in the *Globe* described the scene: "There, in the Middlesex Superior courtroom, stood lawyers from the most powerful firms in Massachusetts, in a tableau that included former US attorneys and White House aides, grandees with pocket kerchiefs and prodigies in power ties." The trial involved so many lawyers, the *Globe* couldn't resist poking fun, nicknaming the proceedings, "the legal full employment act."

It was not a laughing matter for the Demoulas family. The lawsuit involved years of legal wrangling, including affidavits, interrogatories, depositions, and meetings with their legal teams. The trial itself ran a grueling four months during which Telemachus was grilled on the witness stand for seventeen days. The proceedings became so heated that Arthur T., frustrated by the way his father Telemachus was being treated on the stand, and reacting to a comment directed to him by Arthur S., reportedly took a swing at his cousin at the back of the courtroom. Arthur S. did not retaliate, and the scuffle ended as soon as it began. But in the public's eye, the event came to define the animosity between the cousins.

The jury deliberated for thirteen days before making its ruling that May. They found in favor of George's heirs, and Judge Maria Lopez eventually awarded 50.5 percent of the company to Arthur S. and his kin. Lawyers for the winning side estimated the losses at between $500 million to $800 million.

Telemachus, seventy-three at the time, wasn't even in the courtroom on the day the verdict was read: one of his attorneys said he didn't make it because he was working at the time. "He was in the produce section arranging the oranges," an employee would later tell a reporter.

The suit expanded into a litany of related court battles over the years. There were accusations on both sides. All were reported extensively in the media. Telemachus's side accused Arthur S. of trying to influence the judge in the case and in fact filed multiple recusal motions to have her removed from the case. They also claimed that listening devices were planted in Market Basket's corporate offices to secretly learn about Telemachus's trial strategy. George's heirs countered the bugging case with still another suit—this one alleging that Telemachus's side had violated their fiduciary duties by making real-estate loans to business associates and friends using the funds in the profit-sharing account. They wanted Telemachus, Arthur T., and a third trustee of the plan, D. Harold Sullivan, removed as trustees of the profit-sharing plan—they were ultimately not successful.

Sadly, family relations had long passed the point where there was any hope of reconciliation. Even a family tragedy could not mend the wounds. George's son Evan died in a car crash in Montreal in 1993. He was only thirty-eight, and his wife, Rafaele, was pregnant with their first child. Lawyers for George's side called Telemachus's family and friends and told them not to attend the funeral. John, the oldest brother of George and Telemachus, was turned away at the door. Severed family ties have never mended.

—

In 2003, Telemachus contracted an illness that quickly led to complications. He was treated at Massachusetts General Hospital where he died shortly afterwards at age eighty-two. The obituary in the *Boston Globe* read simply, "Telemachus Demoulas, supermarket giant." A thousand people attended his funeral, with hundreds of others waiting in a nearly two-hour-long line to enter the Holy Trinity Greek Orthodox Church. More than a hundred students at the nearby affiliated Hellenic American Academy waved American and Greek flags as they waited for the funeral procession to pass. Telemachus had been a major supporter of both the church and its school and went to church there every Sunday, often alone.

Telemachus's death was the end of a chapter in the company's growth. It also opened a new chapter, one that pitted two starkly different philosophies against one another. These competing philosophies about whom a company is meant to serve belonged to Telemachus's son Arthur T. Demoulas and George's son Arthur S. Demoulas. It was a rivalry between cousins that began a march toward the protests of 2014.

3

"Learn the Business, Young Man"

A popular image displayed at the rallies and in Market Basket stores during the 2014 protest borrowed imagery from Barack Obama's 2008 presidential campaign. The iconic poster designed by Shepard Fairey shows Obama staring pensively and using a Warhol-esque mix of muted blues and reds; the words "HOPE" or "BELIEVE" were typically written below. Market Basket protesters abstracted a photo of Arthur T. in similar fashion. The image popped up on posters at stores across the chain at rallies and in car windows. It became a ubiquitous reminder of the man protesters were fighting for. The picture gave Arthur T. a mystical quality that only grew over the weeks of the conflict.

Long before the protest of 2014, Arthur T. had developed a reputation for being a generous person and an unassuming executive. Stories from associates and customers circulated of how he helped those less fortunate through charitable giving. While visiting stores, he has been known to help customers load groceries from their shopping carriages into their cars. He assisted associates with emergency medical bills. When an employee was grieving a tragic death in the family, Arthur T. would appear at the funeral. Incredibly, it can seem as though everyone working at Market Basket has a story of a time that Arthur T. helped him or her in a time of need.

Arthur T. also has outstanding interpersonal skills. These skills are most evident during one-on-one conversations, where he listens attentively. Associates and customers say that he hardly ever forgets a face or a name. After meeting him once, the next time they see him—say, bumping into him during one of his store visits—he not only will address them by name but may also ask how their daughter—and he will remember her name as well—is doing in school or whether their father had his surgery yet.

Newspapers and television stations threw fuel on the fire, crafting a narrative of Arthur T. as the benevolent superhero. Coverage was generally very favorable but also somewhat simplistic. James Post, a retired professor of management at Boston University says, "I think much of that is clearly warranted." But he also notes that part of that image was thrust upon him because he came to represent a larger ideal; some of the adulation is "projection," he says. These stories illuminate an important side to Arthur T., but they fall short of capturing his full character, especially as a manager.

A deeper look at Arthur T. Demoulas reveals a more interesting and complex man. He is humble and soft-spoken but also a perfectionist who demands excellence. He takes his work seriously and leads by example. He is generous in sometimes surprising ways but can also be a hardnosed negotiator, not willing to give an inch—or a dime. You won't ever see him outside of his signature suit and tie, and the tie is likely to be the same maroon color worn by store directors at Market Basket. Although he has a formal aspect to his nature, he comes across as genuine and personable. He is not the kind of executive who tries to dominate a conversation or tries to force a firm handshake on someone to make an impression. Rather, he is a listener who gives people his complete attention, looking them straight in the eye when they speak. Underlying his low-key demeanor, however, there is a quiet nervousness. It's as if he knows that somewhere, in one of his stores, there is a pallet that needs to be unloaded, a can of soup to be stocked, or a customer to be rung through. He is a man of many talents, but like the rest of us, has flaws and probably a few regrets. More than anything, Arthur T. is a man who is admired by thousands and appears to sincerely love his work and the people he works with. He is an integral piece in the Market Basket puzzle.

Those who work closely with Arthur T. paint a portrait of him as a good person, one defined by both generosity and integrity. According to these accounts, his integrity is that of a man who tries to be honest with himself and with the facts. His associates say that when media reports concentrate too much on his generous side, they overlook his management philosophy. It is a philosophy that has contributed to a period of historic growth for the company. It is also one that conflicts sharply with that of Arthur S., his cousin.

—

The protest in 2014 was the culmination of a longtime struggle between Arthur T. and Arthur S. over control of Market Basket. That struggle went beyond dollars and cents, and even beyond the family quarrels over the years. At the root of the conflict are two very different understandings of whom a company is meant to serve.

Arthur T. puts service to customers, employees, and suppliers first. He believes that a manager's role is to nurture a culture and design a set of practices that benefits them; if this is done successfully, shareholders will benefit as a consequence. Arthur S., in contrast, takes the view that shareholders should come first; a manager's primary responsibility is to maximize profits for shareholders, which in theory is aligned with the goals of customers, employees, and others. These are fundamentally different ways of thinking that do not coexist well.

Where did Arthur T. and Arthur S. Demoulas develop their respective mind-sets? For both, the answer can be found, at least in part, in their formative years of the 1970s, 1980s, and 1990s.

—

Arthur Telemachus Demoulas was born in 1955, the only son of four children. As the first son in a Greek family, he was naturally given the name of his grandfather. Unlike his parents and grandparents, Arthur T. grew up in a well-to-do family. During his childhood, his father Telemachus and uncle George had already expanded the business to more than a dozen stores, and the Demoulas family was quite well known around Lowell. The family moved to Andover while Arthur T. was in high school.

Still, many at Andover High didn't know just how well off Arthur's family was. He did not flaunt his wealth. At a party the family hosted one winter, Patty Healy-Osborne, who graduated the year after Arthur, noticed that her classmate flipped a switch to turn on heaters under the driveway to melt snow that began falling. "It was the first time I realized this down-to-earth guy came from financial means. You would never know it," she said.

Arthur T.'s first victories came on the playing field. He was active in the fall, winter, and spring seasons, playing football, hockey, and track for Andover High School. His tenacity brought him success on the gridiron despite his small size: he stands at five feet, five inches. In his senior year (1972–1973), Arthur T. was one of the top running backs in the Merrimack Valley League. (Coincidentally, his cousin Evan was a top running back at Dracut High.) Arthur T. ran for 277 yards and added 78 receiving yards and 2 touchdowns that year. His team went 8–1, better than any previous Andover team.

Two former teammates from that year said they weren't surprised at the devotion Arthur T. has attracted as the head of Market Basket. The respect Arthur T. showed for his teammates on the Golden Warriors was the same he showed his colleagues at Market Basket years later, said Scott Seero, the team's quarterback. "Nobody worked harder in the off-season, was more courageous and was a better teammate. He was all about the success of the team . . . He was as great of a person as he was a football player, and he was a damn good football player."

"He's that type of guy whose kindness exceeds everything and who generates trust and optimism," said Ray Pizarro, who was a defensive lineman.

Throughout Arthur T.'s childhood, he bagged oranges, stacked shelves, deboned chicken, and performed other chores typical of operating a grocery store. Importantly, he developed an enthusiasm to learn the business. His father had built a company and a culture that Arthur T. admired and already felt a strong loyalty to. Arthur T. wanted to continue that tradition and contribute to that culture. Telemachus was pleased to see his son's interest in the business and encouraged him, but he took a characteristically tough stance. His attitude was always, "You want to learn the business, young man? You start at the bottom."

In his teenage years, Arthur T. worked in the warehouse unloading goods from trailers. After that, he worked as a sacker in the stores. Then he worked as a clerk. It wasn't easy moving into positions as the boss's son, but he tried to concentrate on his duties, being the best clerk and food merchant he could be. The jobs were as demanding as they are today, but he got little sympathy from his father—just more reminders of "learn the business, young man."

Arthur T. showed remarkable maturity for a high school student. He was obviously being groomed to take over the company, but he seemed to take nothing for granted. "In the summer, Artie was working," says Scott Seero. "He wasn't on vacation—he was working hard to learn the family business. He didn't drive a Mercedes or have a driver or anything like that. He was just one of the boys."

Even after joining the board of directors just a year out of high school in 1974, he kept an even keel. Arthur T. was steadied by a true love for the grocery business.

It is unusual for the son of a CEO to work so many nonmanagement jobs. It is even more unusual for a member of the board of directors to do so. This gave Arthur T. an uncommon perspective. One day, he would evaluate a proposal as a board member. The next day, he might serve someone at the deli counter. Not only did this keep him grounded, but it also gave him immediate feedback on how the decisions of upper management were affecting individual people working or shopping in the stores. Making this link is now a hallmark of his management approach.

As Arthur T. grew into management positions, Telemachus began to imprint some of his management style on his boy. He told Arthur T. to judge each person individually based on personal experience, not hearsay. He advised him that to get to know someone, he would have to "sit down and talk to them" and then ask himself, "Is he honest and sincere?" said family friend Bill Poulios.

Telemachus continued to instill toughness and independence in his son. He wanted to empower Arthur T. to make decisions and solve problems on his own. According to Poulios, Telemachus didn't tolerate Arthur T. bringing him issues that he was perfectly capable of address-ing on his own. "I don't want to hear about problems; you settle it," he instructed. "People who are in charge, they settle problems, that's what bosses do." Poulios said Telemachus also taught Arthur T. to "go easy on [his] spending." That accent on efficiency is still central to the company.

Arthur T. continued his ascent in the company. He eventually took full executive responsibility as the president and CEO in 2008.

—

One man who has seen Arthur T.'s development from a young age is William Marsden, currently a director of operations at Market Basket. Marsden joined the company in 1957 and became "the right-hand man" to Telemachus Demoulas. Today, he is one of Arthur T.'s most trusted and seasoned advisors. He is respected across the company; almost everyone refers to him as Mr. Marsden, not Bill. Most senior managers name him as a mentor and say they are thankful for his guidance. These managers often say that they learned the most from Marsden when he told them things they *didn't* want to hear, when he challenged them to confront their biases and make a better decision. It's a form of intellectual courage that Marsden holds dear.

Like others, Marsden is somewhat bemused by one-sided depic-tions of Arthur T. that have emerged in the media over the past couple of years. "All I've heard is that he's a nice guy," he says. He agrees that, first and foremost, Arthur T. is a "good person" who puts the company first. But it frustrates Marsden that many have overlooked his skill at the helm of Market Basket. "He can be charming, but let there be no misunderstanding," says Marsden. "He is a very astute manager." In fact, Marsden says, "I don't find him to be so nice *all the time*." Arthur T. can be "difficult to deal with" because he has a "tremendous ability to dig away at the facts and get the accurate facts." This approach can be especially disconcerting to those who have not done their homework before making a proposal to him.

A defining characteristic that emerges when colleagues talk about Arthur T. is his desire, and uncanny ability, to visualize how executive decisions will ultimately affect an individual person. When he receives proposals from members of his team or when he evaluates a new million-dollar deal, his questions tend to be detail oriented; he wants to make sure that thinking is never too abstract. How will that proposal make the experience better for a customer walking into the Burlington store this morning? How will the proposal affect the duties of an associate working in the warehouse?

Consider an example. When choosing a location for a new store, other managers might gauge the revenue potential in the area based on population. They might then analyze that revenue potential against the cost of opening and operating the store. A more inquisitive manager might also inquire about the income level of consumers in the area and which competitors are nearby. But this is where many top-level executives would end their analysis, leaving it to others to fill in the gaps. In contrast, Arthur T. seems to revel in these details. He always goes deeper. For instance, he might ask, "What entrance ramp will a customer use if they are driving East on Route 44?" Due diligence for him and his management team means doing the work to find connections between multimillion-dollar decisions and the experience of a single person.

A supermarket has so many moving parts: imagine millions of items, each being shipped by hundreds of vendors, handled by dozens of associates in multiple locations over a period of days, and then assorted in the right way on the shelves so that millions of customers have them available when they want them. It's easy to get lost in the details. This extreme focus on how big decisions impact an individual is one way that Market Basket keeps from being distracted. When William Marsden describes this approach, he says, "I don't like the word simple because it's not a simple company, but we try to keep it as *uncomplicated* as we possibly can." By consistently asking how individuals will be affected, it makes decisions more intellectually challenging, but the result is often a streamlined, uncomplicated operation that functions well.

Marsden says that Arthur T. took the best from both his mother and father. From his mother, Irene, he took his thoughtful nature. She is "kind and sincere" and one who "always made you feel part of the family." Telemachus was giving in his own way but was a difficult taskmaster. He was widely loved, but he had a strong personality that instilled discipline, respect, and sometimes fear. Associates recall leaving his office trembling after Telemachus chastised them for not thinking through something carefully enough. It was the style of a boss of his generation. Arthur T., on the other hand, is perhaps better suited to today's workplace. He is equally demanding but is also more of a listener. Associates *seek* his opinion. "He is a magnet," Marsden says.

Marsden recalls that when Telemachus would visit a store or review a proposal, he would focus on things that others might consider minutia. In the store, he would spot a misplaced carton of milk or notice that sackers were not filling grocery bags full enough, wasting two cents because they would have to use an extra bag. Telemachus was a ruthless cost cutter in some areas but was very generous in others, investing savings in the business. For example, he insisted that millions of dollars in earnings go to the profit-sharing and retirement plans he implemented. His goal was to run an efficient business that takes care of its people. He once told Marsden, "[Money is] not what drives me. I want to be a good merchant. That's all I want."

While their day-to-day interactions are quite different in tone, Arthur T.'s larger goals stray little from those of his father. By most accounts, Arthur T.'s overarching goal is to grow the company, and his personal goal is to be a good merchant. Arthur T. describes these goals articulately in some board meetings. At one meeting in 2010, he introduced himself to Nabil El-Hage, a new director at the time, by stating his priorities as an executive. Arthur T.'s central contention was that serving customers well would always result in rewards for shareholders but that rewarding shareholders first can sometimes make it difficult to serve customers well. "I want you to know how I think," he said. "The customers come first. The associates of the company come [next]. The communities are now our social responsibility, and then the shareholders."

Arthur T. isn't one for academic jargon, but he was describing the tenets of stakeholder theory, a view of how companies operate that has been quietly growing a following among management scholars. Stakeholder theorists believe that companies are best viewed as a system to create value. They warn that placing shareholder interests above others can lead to a vicious cycle of chasing profits at the expense of stakeholders, such as customers and vendors.

It is an approach that stands in stark contrast to the one held by Arthur T.'s cousin and rival in the Market Basket drama, Arthur S. Demoulas.

—

Arthur Stephen Demoulas was born three years after Arthur T., the youngest of his four siblings. In their youth, the two played together on the streets of Lowell and then Andover, Massachusetts. They would trick-or-treat together each Halloween as part of the larger Demoulas clan that included Arthur S.'s older brother Evan. Like his cousin, Arthur S. played football and hockey. He excelled at hockey, attending the University of Maine where he played as a defenseman in the team's inaugural season.

This, however, is where versions of his life begin to diverge. Although he continued to work at Market Basket throughout college, there is disagreement about how committed he was to the family the biggest of which was opening a grocery in the first place. This tolerance for risk taking and thinking on one's own was passed down to Telemachus and George and then to Arthur T. and other grandchildren. Post says that Arthur T. has not "lost sight of the fact that he is the grandson of people who were immigrant grocers; that's the blood line." And that bloodline fed a self-reliance that endures.

Another source of the company's unconventional thinking is the population that it serves and draws upon for associates. The company has always operated in communities with predominantly middle- and low-income families. In the early days, it was mill workers. When the mills moved away, the jobs of these populations changed somewhat, but the mind-set remained. It is a mind-set that values street smarts as much as any textbook knowledge. In many of these communities, you won't find many people with MBAs or PhDs. According to the US Census, only 22 percent of Lowell residents have a bachelor's degree. Compare that to Boston where 44 percent of the population has a bachelor's degree or higher. Obviously, many people in these communities would like to attend college but can't because of poor finances or other reasons. But there remains, in some quarters, a sense that much of the textbook knowledge about business is impractical and irrelevant. (This view is shared by some academics; an article in the *Harvard Business Review* accused business schools of failing to teach useful skills and instill ethical thinking.) It is people from these communities that join Market Basket as part-time baggers and work their way into management positions. Many gain tremendous knowledge about business but remain skeptical of textbook solutions.

A final source of the unconventional thinking at Market Basket is the practice of promoting from within. Other companies recruit at the finest business schools. An employee at one of these companies could see their hopes of promotion disappear when a position they have been eying is taken by a recent MBA graduate. When companies place such a high value on degrees, it tends to fuel a race to build one's resume.

In contrast, Market Basket does not recruit from business schools. The company does receive many applications from MBA graduates.

But these candidates quickly become discouraged when they realize how strongly Market Basket holds to its hire-from-within philosophy; the candidate would have to start where everyone else in the company started, bagging groceries or pushing shopping carriages.

Moreover, promotions at Market Basket are not based on seniority. Senior managers say they give promotions strictly on merit. While the years an associate has served the company is valued, it is rarely the basis for advancement. The system is a bit like how one advances in some of the martial arts; one gets promoted to the next color belt after demonstrating mastery of the techniques at the current level.

By promoting only from within and strictly based on merit, associates know that the only way to get ahead is to demonstrate their ability to solve problems and seize opportunities. They know that a potential promotion will not be snatched up by an outsider with an advanced degree; their competition is in plain sight: it is the clerk in the next aisle or the store director down the street. The sense of family makes this a somewhat friendly competition, but it is intense nonetheless. Associates prove themselves by finding a novel way to help the company serve customers better.

Overall, the company's history, the communities in which it operates, and the practice of promoting from within all contribute to a culture that values unconventional thinking, even as it retains a conservative veneer.

—

No one personifies the desire to break with common wisdom more than Tom Trainor, a Market Basket district supervisor. Trainor is a straight talker in the classic mold. While he speaks deliberately, he prides himself on being able to look a person in the eye and tell him or her how he sees it. One gets the sense that he feels it would simply be a waste of everyone's time to sugarcoat anything. At rallies in the summer, he borrowed language from the Boston Bruins fans who say, "Don't poke the bear." He meant that the Market Basket family is not to be reckoned with. But he carries that same intensity at a personal level. You don't want to poke Tom Trainor unless you have good reason.

Trainor has held strong convictions from a young age. He was a good student in high school and was accepted to the University of Lowell (now the University of Massachusetts, Lowell) with a full merit scholarship. The university wanted students like him.

Throughout four years of high school and into the first two years of college, he worked at Market Basket. He loved the excitement and the challenge of it. He was "bitten" by the grocery business.

As he thought about returning to university for his junior year, Trainor began to see a disconnect. He was learning in his classes, but they were not getting him any closer to his real passion. He had another calling, and it was the grocery business. It didn't seem to make sense to delay the inevitable.

Even then, Trainor was the kind of person who liked to go "all in." At age twenty, he announced to his parents that he would quit university and make a career at Market Basket. Not surprisingly, his parents thought the idea was foolhardy. But Trainor stuck to his convictions. He explained that this was his passion, and he was already being recognized by his superiors for his hard work and initiative. Furthermore, the company was "rock solid." There was a future there.

It isn't clear whether his parents came around to his way of thinking or simply realized that he was too stubborn to change his mind. But they supported his decision, and he never looked back. He moved from being a part-time bagger to being a part-time clerk in the grocery. Then he went full-time, working as a grocery manager, head cashier, assistant store director, and then store director at several stores.

Today Trainor oversees about half of Market Basket's stores.

Not long after he was promoted to become the store director of the Salem, New Hampshire, store (#31), he was approached by Telemachus Demoulas.

"I haven't seen [your store] yet, have I?" said Demoulas.

"No sir, you haven't yet," replied Trainor.

As he answered, Trainor was already thinking of all the work that had to be done before a visit would pass muster with Mr. D.

Demoulas made it a point to visit stores regularly. He typically got to each store a couple of times each year. During those visits, Demoulas was merciless. He looked at every detail. He held back nothing, and he demanded perfection.

Within a month, Trainor got a call from a colleague at the nearby Methuen store. Mr. D. had just arrived for a store visit; his next stop was probably Salem. He had no more than two hours to make any last-minute preparations.

But Trainor wasn't concerned. His store was in perfect condition. "We looked absolutely pristine, like a grand opening."

Telemachus greeted Trainor warmly and then started walking the floor. The inspection began. In those days, there were no refrigerated endcaps, and most Market Basket stores would pile apples and pears on tables. Telemachus asked why the fruit was outside of refrigeration. Trainor was a bit tongue-tied. He answered, "That's what the other stores are doing."

This was not the type of answer that was going to satisfy Telemachus. The next few hours were devoted to resetting the entire produce department. Once he felt things were moving in the right direction, Telemachus turned to Trainor:

"Did you learn anything today, young man?"

"Yes, Mr. D."

"Well, tell me what you learned."

"I learned that in this store, I need to think out of the box."

Trainor now recalls, "He turned around, walked out of the store and left me in a pile of peanuts that he had thrown on the floor from another display. You look back on it and laugh now, but he was teaching me how to manage my own store. And not [do something] because everybody else did it." Trainor never forgot it.

Years later, when Trainor was already in charge of his third store, he was still trying to look at things from a novel perspective. At that time, Market Basket started selling shrimp platters. But since shrimp needs to be refrigerated, stores had to hide them behind glass doors. Customers weren't noticing the new product. So Trainor took some wooden bins from the grocery counter and filled them with ice, creating makeshift displays in the aisle where they would be more enticing for customers. It worked. Sales were brisk, and he received accolades from executives for his initiative. Before he knew it, other Market Basket stores were finding similar ways of displaying their shrimp. A small innovation improved sales across the whole company.

This is how a lot of innovations develop, Trainor says. "Somebody in the store, whether it be a department head, or it could be a full-time clerk, comes up with an idea. You have to be open minded to people's ideas."

—

As the above example shows, thinking unconventionally can lead to coming up with ideas before competitors do. But it can also help a manager resist the temptation to blindly follow competitors. Consider the company's approach to loyalty cards.

Those who study customer loyalty find the 80/20 rule to be fairly reliable. The idea is that customers vary widely, with some customers being more valuable to the company than others. For many companies, approximately 80 percent of profits come from approximately 20 percent of customers. As a result, many companies work very hard to identify whether you and I are part of that 20 percent. If they think we are, we'll likely get even more deals in the hopes that we never defect to a competitor. A common way to track this purchasing behavior is by offering rewards cards or credit cards that help them link each person's purchase over months or years. You'll notice cards like these at places such as T. J. Maxx, Amazon, Starbucks, and Best Buy. These stores must prioritize customers. Otherwise, they would spend too much effort and money trying to service low-profit customers and not enough to retain high-profit customers.

The grocery business is a bit different, however, and Market Basket is even more so. A large number of Market Basket customers do all their weekly shopping at the chain. This means that there are tens of thousands, maybe hundreds of thousands, of customers who purchase on the order of $100–$250 worth of groceries per week. Each family is unique in terms of *what* it purchases, but a very large proportion of its customer base has a similar value in terms of profitability.

Market Basket recognizes this and has broken with the retail trend of tracking the purchases of each family. You don't see rewards cards at Market Basket. The company does not try to create tiers of customers because distinctions between customers would not be meaningful. Market Basket gives the same deals and the same level of service to everyone, regardless of background or family income. Throughout 2014, the company offered a chain-wide 4 percent discount on every purchase; incredibly, the discount was calculated at the register after all other sales and coupons.

One Market Basket associate suggests that the cards represent a nonsensical offer in which customers need to give a card to get a deal; he says that customers would think, "Well, why can't you just give me the better price without the loyalty card? Why do you need my phone number and other personal information?" Market Basket associates see these programs as intrusive, unnecessary, and somewhat disingenuous. Unlike competitors that alter their pricing based on the household incomes of families in each zip code, Market Basket offers the same pricing for all customers in all stores, whether in Cape Cod, Massachusetts; Haverhill, Massachusetts; or Rochester, New Hampshire.

Somewhat surprisingly, this approach has two benefits for Market Basket. First, it reduces the overhead costs associated with running a rewards card program. Analyzing the data alone costs some companies millions in salary and technology expenses.

More important, the egalitarian treatment contributes to customer loyalty. Some of these customers are tiered out of the best deals and services at other retailers. At Market Basket, customers finally feel that they have found a place where they receive the respect they deserve. Sidestepping rewards cards and other tracking is an unconventional practice that pays off because it fits with Market Basket's situation and business model.

—

If you are looking to find a listing of store locations and weekly specials online, you need to visit mydemoulas.com where you'll find a modest website. But this website is not owned or managed by the company. It was started by Michael Devaney, a customer who, after struggling to keep up with sale items, decided to take matters into his own hands. He now runs the unofficial Demoulas website as his full-time job out of his home in Concord, New Hampshire.

"It handles the traffic," Devaney said. "People love it. And I like them to be on the site because I built it. And I feel proud of it, you know?"

He sees his main job as posting weekly circulars and coupons. But over time, his site has grown, and he now provides store locations, deli menus, and other information. He even has a section on the history of the company. Traffic has boomed to 1.2 million unique visitors per month, an astounding amount for a one-person website.

Clearly, there is a demand for information about Market Basket. However, to date, the company has felt that the costs involved outweigh the benefit. Carrying a professionally run website would be expensive. In addition, senior management has limited expertise in having an Internet presence. Hosting a website might also contradict the notion of a person serving a person, which is important to Arthur T. Demoulas.

Some are shocked that a massive company that is so sophisticated in other realms would not yet have a website. The conscious decision to depart from the pack speaks volumes about the culture of originality at Market Basket. "If I could have it any way," Devaney said, "I would love for Market Basket to buy my website, relieve me of my duty, and for them to take it over." If Market Basket ever does launch a site, it is likely that it won't look a lot like those of Shaw's and Hannaford.

PART THREE

Throughout the summer of 2014, the Market Basket protest was front-page news nearly every day. The *Boston Globe* dedicated more than a dozen reporters to the story. Television news provided daily updates. Coverage reached as far as New Zealand. Google tracked eighty to one hundred articles per week on Market Basket during these six weeks; normally there are but a handful.

Despite extensive coverage, the media struggled to find a simple way to describe what was happening at Market Basket.

Was it a strike? Very few employees had actually walked off the job. The vast majority remained on the job, albeit with reduced hours and a nonexistent workload.

Was it a labor dispute? Associates were nonunion, and moreover, the dispute involved managers and executives, people who are not traditionally considered "labor."

Was it a boycott? Yes, but normally boycotts are meant to show displeasure. This boycott was a display of support for the company.

The events defied description. "We don't know what to call it either," said Jim Fantini, a vendor who had assumed a role as one of the point people for the "Save Market Basket" page on Facebook as well as the We Are Market Basket blog.

This was an act of civil disobedience, not against a government, but in order to save a beloved company. It was a sort of "corporate disobedience."

Whatever the term, everyone agreed that this movement was unprecedented. What had begun with a small group a year before had, by the end of August 2014, grown to touch nearly everyone in Massachusetts and New Hampshire. During this period, the protest was a topic of conversation in the workplaces, banks, and main street boutiques of quaint New England towns. People across the region knew that thousands of people's livelihoods were at risk. They feared that this could be the end of a company many considered to be an old friend.

At every stage of this protest, the distinctive pillars of the Market Basket culture provided a foundation for the protest to take flight and ultimately become successful. Its culture of service to the community, its sense of family and empowerment, and its unconventional solutions to problems provided the movement with the motivation, unity, and resourcefulness it needed to succeed.

8

"A Predetermined Assault"

The battle for Market Basket started, simply enough, with a change of heart for a single minority shareholder. That shareholder was Rafaela Evans, the widow of Arthur S.'s brother Evan Demoulas. Though by 2013, she lived in Europe and had only distant ties to the Demoulas family, it was her decision that led to a domino effect that changed Market Basket forever.

Only nine individuals owned shares of the company—all descendants, or in-laws of descendants, of two brothers: George and Telemachus Demoulas. When Evan Demoulas, one of George's sons, died in a car accident in 1993, his widow and his daughter inherited his shares. Though she was rarely heard from, Rafaele Evans played a pivotal role. The heirs of Telemachus controlled 49.5 percent of the company, while Evans and her daughter's shares combined at around 15 percent of the company. Evans admired Arthur T.'s skill as an executive and for years gave his side her support, forming a sort of majority coalition.

Then, almost inexplicably, she changed her mind.

—

For more than a decade preceding the protests, the board of directors at Market Basket consisted of seven members. The two so-called A directors represented the interests of George's heirs. Arthur S. was one of these directors. Two "B directors" represented Telemachus's heirs. The remaining three directors, called "A/B directors," were to be independent and were meant to take a more advisory role, dispassionately settling disputes when necessary. Of course, these independent directors were chosen by the shareholders, and whoever controlled a majority share had additional influence in appointing an A/B director if they chose to wield it.

So it was that as the board turned over, Arthur S. and George's other heirs wrestled control of the independent directors away from Arthur T. and his three sisters. While Rafaele Evans had switched allegiances sometime prior, it was not until new independent directors were instated in 2013 that her influence fully materialized.

A director loyal to Arthur T. described it this way: "The shift [of Rafaela Evans] portended the ascendancy of the non-working half of the Demoulas family to corporate control and satisfaction for their pent-up lust for cash. That drive was apparently insufficiently attended to during the decade that the operating side of the family . . . had reinvested some of the profits of the company toward growth and survival in an increasingly cutthroat industry." Translated, Arthur S.'s side of the family now controlled the board of directors. The board moved to shift more liquidity to the shareholders, and as the *Wall Street Journal* noted, they were "banding together to remove the CEO." Keith Cowan, a former executive at Sprint Nextel living in Atlanta, shifted from one of Arthur S.'s A directors to an independent A/B director, also taking the role of chairman. Arthur S. took Cowan's vacated seat and resumed his role as an A director. Gerard Levins, a Boston-based tax attorney, continued as an A director. The two additional A/B seats were taken by Ron Weiner, president of an accounting and consulting firm in New York City, and Nabil El-Hage, a strategy and finance consultant who once taught at Harvard Business School (El-Hage stepped down from the board in 2013 and was replaced by Eric Gebaide, a managing director of a boutique investment banking firm in New York City).

In 2013, as spring moved into summer, it became apparent that despite the recent successes of the company, the revamped board was bent on removing Arthur T. from his post as CEO. He sensed that it wanted to take the company in another direction, one that was at odds with the model and culture he and his father had shaped over decades.

Around this time, Arthur S., through a member of his team, attempted to turn up the heat by approaching the *Boston Globe* with accusations that Arthur T. was not fit for the role of CEO. Arthur S. had filed a lawsuit in June 2013 and attached the first meeting agenda to his pleading in order to publicize that the board intended to remove Arthur T. The *Globe* contacted a person close to Arthur T.'s team of advisors for a comment on the allegation. When he learned of the *Globe*'s inquiry, Arthur T. realized that the dispute with Arthur S. was going to take on a more public profile.

Arthur T. next granted interviews to the *Globe* and the *Lowell Sun*. One of us (Welker) was at the *Sun* for this interview. Arthur T. sat at the end of the table, wearing his trademark suit with white shirt and maroon tie. He and some of his top managers took reporters through the facts of what Market Basket had accomplished during his five-year tenure. Sales had risen from $2.4 billion to more than $4 billion. The employee base had grown from fourteen thousand full- or part-time jobs to about twenty-two thousand, but payroll took up a smaller share of sales—about 10.4 percent—than when he began as CEO. The margin topped 8 percent, exceeding the average for regional or national grocers of all sizes. They reviewed the recent shareholder history and said his prized profit-sharing program—started by his father in 1963—was at risk. In 2012, the plan had dispersed $20 million to retired Market Basket workers. It had more than $500 million on hand.

Then Arthur T. made his case on a more personal level. He spoke of the culture at Market Basket, that he was committed to maintaining and deepening that sense at Market Basket of human beings serving other human beings. He also spoke of the importance that the company holds in the community by serving low-income customers in ways that others don't, of teenagers who arrive with few skills and leave as polished young professionals.

He described Market Basket as so many others do: as a family. "We have a family feel in this organization," he said. Associates at all levels view Market Basket as a two-way lifetime commitment. Some hope, as Arthur T. himself no doubt does, that when they retire, Market Basket will have been the only company they ever worked for. "If they remove me," he asked, "what kind of message is that to the company?"

Arthur T. described his expected firing as a "predetermined assault."

When asked why the rivaling faction of the company and the directors they appointed would want to get rid of him, Arthur T. said he was eager to hear their justification. Of course, he did know their central allegations against him—that some shareholders accused him of reckless spending. They also claimed that Arthur T. was not being transparent enough and that he was involved in too many dealings with relatives. Arthur S. and other directors characterized the expected vote as an attempt at better accountability. The board was especially focused on the generous profit-sharing plan and additional bonuses to employees.

In contrast, Arthur T. saw bonuses and profit sharing as an investment, not an expense. "If that's reckless spending," he said, "I'm guilty."

—

On July 10, 2013, Arthur T. called a meeting of all his senior managers. It was not terribly unusual for Arthur T. to address the full team. But some managers sensed that this meeting was different. He took the additional step of calling in those who were on their day off.

They assembled in the lunchroom. Arthur T. began the meeting. He informed the managers that he wanted them to know from him that the board had changed membership and that a major item on those newest members' agenda was to fire and replace him as CEO. After the announcement, Arthur T. left the meeting.

The room was silent at first. It was a scene of shock and disbelief. How could a board remove a CEO who had such a strong track record over seven years? Managers believed they had a winning business model and that the company was just hitting its stride. Add to that their personal loyalty to the man, and incredulity shifted toward infuriation. They needed to be heard.

Tom Trainor was one of the many managers who stood up during a postannouncement discussion among the team. He remembers suggesting that they go to the board, in numbers, to show the board how much loyalty Arthur T. had from associates. "Surely they'd be smart enough to understand that if store directors and senior managers showed up [to the next board meeting], there's got to be a reason for it," he recalls thinking.

The next board meeting was the following week, eight days later. Trainor wanted to get the word out "that next Thursday, we're gonna be there." He reached out to people he trusted most. One of these was vendor Jim Fantini. Fantini agreed that Arthur T. needed their help and decided to work with Trainor to gather as many voices as possible. They took to social media.

Trainor opened a Facebook account under the name "Save Market Basket." Wading into the social media world felt out of place for Trainor. He was comfortable with Market Basket's technology but had never had a personal Facebook account himself—he still doesn't. At the time, he didn't know that the "wall" or "timeline" was the key place that users post messages and see the messages of others. He had to learn everything from the ground up, often by asking his daughters for help. It was trial and error, but he knew that most associates were technology savvy and that they needed a central place for associates to gather.

Fantini's wife, Nicole, who designs websites, helped him purchase a couple of key URLs (wearemarketbasket.com and savemarketbasket.com) and configure them to work together. They wanted to make sure that the various inroads to their social media were integrated enough that if a person arrived at one site, they would naturally get to one of the others. This way, their social media presence was more likely to build on itself.

There was a sense of urgency, and Fantini and Trainor were willing to give almost anything a try. Fantini's wife recalled seeing petition sites that helped track signatures for just about any cause. "Why don't you start a petition," she asked. They agreed and put their full weight behind it. Treating this like a store promotion for a product, they set a goal. They figured that given the short time frame and the number of employees, five hundred online signatures made sense. They hoped at least to get a few hundred. They set up the petition page and posted notices on the Facebook page to encourage people to sign it. At least one store printed and distributed cards inviting associates and customers to join the petition.

A few hours after opening the account, they checked the total. They had reached about ten signatures. Fantini crossed his fingers and went to bed. The next morning he awoke to ten thousand signatures. "It just exploded," he says. By the following Thursday, when the board meeting was to take place, they had more than forty-five thousand. "That got the social, the people part of it, started," Fantini says.

Social media would continue to bear fruit for protesters. "We tapped into something," Fantini says. "It gave people a voice in the fight, an avenue to get the news about it, and to express their views about it." Person by person, a force was building.

—

As the board meeting neared, analysts questioned why a leadership shakeup was necessary when the company had solid performance in recent years. Neil Stern of the retail consultant McMillan Doolittle called Market Basket "one of the real success stories," adding, "You wonder, why rock the boat now?"

Others worried that the move could damage the company permanently. Family business experts saw the company's entwined reputation with the Demoulas family as a double-edged sword. Market Basket and the family were synonymous in many people's minds. Some shoppers still say that they shop at Demoulas decades after the family name was dropped in favor of "Market Basket" as the company moniker.

Jeffrey Davis, a cofounder of the Family Business Association and president of the consulting group Mage LLC, said the Demoulas squabbles were an example of how, especially among successful, multigenerational family businesses, fighting can derail a company's progress or hurt its image. "It's very hard to build a family business and it's very easy to destroy it," he said. And reflecting on whether another CEO could step in with the same success of Arthur T., he said, "Lightning doesn't always strike twice."

Still, the board had publicly committed to sacking him. "Now if [they] don't do it, [they] waffled," Ted Clark, the executive director of the Northeastern University Center for Family Business, said of the board members.

When a company battle plays out in public, as it has for Market Basket, it becomes difficult for decision makers to reverse their decisions. Dissension can be healthy, but a fight such as Market Basket's can also be costly. The company has to pay legal bills, hire public relations or communications staff, and have executives take time away from their daily duties to answer questions about the issue.

Most importantly, the looming decision created uncertainty for associates and customers. Those associates fretted that the days of generous bonuses and family atmosphere might be numbered. Customers worried that a move to the textbook business model of high margins and low service would mean less food on the table along with a worse shopping experience.

—

Arthur T. had sparred with Arthur S. and certain other members of the board of directors for years. Board meeting minutes provide a unique window into the differing view between Arthur T. and some directors. In those minutes, some directors took issue with the way Arthur T. interacted with the board. They claimed he was "openly defiant" of the board and had a "dictatorial" management philosophy. They claimed he withheld information from the board, including for a planned store in the small north-central Massachusetts town of Athol. Arthur T. told the board he hadn't disclosed the project, for which Market Basket had already spent $18 million in unspecified costs, because of what he called a sensitive issue with the developer, the town, and the permitting.

Some directors challenged Arthur T.'s authority to make deals without consulting them first. Arthur T. believed that as the CEO, he needed the authority to make deals quickly and that a lengthy approval process could hamper his ability to seize opportunities and be flexible in negotiations. In August 2012, he told the board, "There's only one boss in the company. There's not two. There's not three. There's not five." He argued that the board had "hired [his] management style" and that part of his "style is not to come back to this board and ask for permission. [He is] going to do it."

Consider an exchange between Arthur T. on one side and directors Arthur S. and Gerrard Levins on the other. Arthur T. informs the board of his plans to give employees extraordinary bonuses totaling between $20 million and $40 million. Levins asks when the board would find out how much in bonuses was given. When Arthur T. says he will tell them the first meeting after it happens, Arthur S. becomes agitated. "Not before?" he asks. Arthur T. fires back, "Are you looking for notification, or are you looking to have approval from the board?" Arthur T. goes on to say that compensation of associates should be up to the CEO.

In another exchange on a similar theme, Gerrard Levins argues that the CEO should get approval from the board for deals that are above a set dollar amount. Arthur T. responds that this would impede his ability to be flexible and to pounce on opportunities. Reminiscent of lessons from his father, he says, "I think you have to have some stock in who you're looking at, who you're talking to, your belief in the person, in the individual, your trust and faith, knowing nobody's perfect." He says that although he will make mistakes, his "batting average" remains strong.

It is worth noting that such a disagreement is not atypical at companies. Commonly, overseeing the CEO is part and parcel of a board's job. But each board must determine, on its own, whether it needs to approval large commitments, such as real estate purchases or strategic partnerships. When it comes to the overall level of oversight, boards and the CEO need to negotiate how much is best. Substantive disagreements are normal and even healthy. However, some discussions in these board meetings became more theatrical and revealed animosity between some directors and representatives from management. At least a few times, those meetings devolved into name calling and bickering.

The June 25, 2003, meeting included a tense back and forth between Arthur S. and William Shea, an A/B director appointed by the Arthur T. side of the family. Shea, who at the time was the board chairman, chastises Arthur S. for interrupting others during the meeting. Arthur S. shoots back sarcastically, "I'm so threatened by you, pointing your finger at me." Soon after, Gerrard Levins accuses Shea of being inconsistent. Arthur S. jumps in: "Well, I'll tell you why he's inconsistent. Because you're a liar. That's why you're inconsistent." Later he tells Shea that he is running the board meeting "like a third grade class." At that point, Shea tells the reporter recording the meeting minutes, "Don't take this down." The meeting went into a recess for ten minutes, and the matter was dropped when they returned.

Arthur S. later got into a heated argument with Shea again and with some members of the company's financial team who presented sales figures for the past year. Arthur S. claimed that the financial team was

not concerned enough with the drop in sales at the Chelsea, Massachusetts, store. Arthur S. scuffles with longtime employee Julien Lacourse.
Lacourse says it is due to a bridge being closed. Arthur S. says he is "concerned about our sales being down . . . and if you want to tell me you're
not, then tell me you're not. OK?" Board Chairman Bill Shea tells him to
stop badgering Lacourse. "I'm not badgering. I'm asking legitimate questions." He goes on to say that "it's always fine and dandy when Arthur
gets to ask a question" and accuses the chairman of being out of line. (See
Appendices A, B, and C for transcripts of these three meetings.)

The divide among members of the board appeared irreconcilable. In previously unpublished minutes from a 2003 board meeting, an independent
director reported to the full board on a prior meeting of the board's Compensation Committee. That committee was tasked with evaluating whether
senior managers at Market Basket were being adequately compensated.

While one of these subcommittee meetings went smoothly, another
turned ugly. The subcommittee was divided, with Arthur S. against any
additional bonuses or profit sharing for the senior managers in question.
The director reported that during a disagreement, Arthur S. "became
extremely disruptive, disrespectful, discourteous, and insulting. He
screamed, cursed, called the members 'stupid' and 'ignorant,' accused
[committee members] of being in the pocket of [the senior managers,
and of] being part of a conspiracy."

Concluding, the director told the full board, "I do not intend to call a
meeting of this Compensation Committee again as I will not be a party
to subjecting members of this board to such abuse." We do not know
Arthur S.'s version of the story—in the documents we reviewed he did
not provide an alternative. It is clear, however, that there was a funda-
mental disconnect, and it was becoming personal.

—

Market Basket had long held its board meetings at the Wyndham
Hotel in Andover, a town near its headquarters in Tewksbury. The
hotel was off a long driveway that stretched past industrial lots just off
Interstate 93, and the location would be a boon to Arthur T. supporters for the highly anticipated board meeting a week after Arthur T.'s

meetings with the *Boston Globe* and the *Lowell Sun*. Market Basket tractor-trailers would pass by on the highway, blasting their horns.

The driveway, half a mile long, gave supporters a chance to line up like a gauntlet, booing the rivaling directors—when they were aware of their identities—and cheering others. They swarmed the car in which Arthur T. sat in the front passenger seat, waving at and shaking hands with him through the open window.

Those supporters would end up staying out in the heat—even as temperatures rose past ninety degrees and afternoon thunderstorms threatened—for more than twelve hours waiting to hear word of whether Arthur T. would be kept or fired. "It's the least we can do for someone who's done so much [for us]," one said.

Supporters came from all corners of Market Basket's territory, some by bus. The crowd was large enough that Andover police had to monitor traffic entering Old River Road, which leads to the hotel. Law enforcement also restricted access to the hotel itself. More officers were stationed outside the hotel boardroom. Some supporters said they had sneaked by police by turning their Market Basket shirts inside out to hide the reason they were there and then walking through the woods. Officers became wise to this and began to ask passersby to show their room keys to prove they were guests of the hotel.

The meeting was held behind closed doors. Arthur T.'s four children, along with other family members and supporters, spent much of the day in the hotel lobby awaiting word of a vote. Arthur T. took trips between the boardroom and a meeting room directly off the lobby, which he and his team had secured for the day. As he passed between rooms during breaks in the meeting, he spoke to family, executives, and public relations specialists. He occasionally made time to greet well-wishers. It was clear from his mood at each of the board meeting's breaks that the discussion was heated. At times, he seemed determined, and at others, nearly despondent. This continued late into the evening.

Eventually, Arthur T. and the others emerged. After more than twelve hours, Arthur T. had succeeded in dodging a bullet. He was still the CEO. However, the board did not vote to keep him as the CEO; it had simply taken no action on the matter. Still, for the crowd, it felt like victory.

Arthur T. exchanged hugs and handshakes, appearing more relieved than happy. A few associates picked him up in the air to sit him on their shoulders. He spoke to a large gathering, mostly associates. "I'll never forget you," he shouted. "You're the best. I never want to leave you."

Arthur T. walked past Steve Paulenka's pickup truck, which was parked nearby. It had already been used as a makeshift stage from which associates had made impassioned speeches in support of their CEO. Paulenka turned to Arthur T.: "One day, maybe not this week or this month, but one day, you're going to give your victory speech from the back of this truck."

In a statement released through the company, Arthur T. said he was "pleased" with the result and hoped to work "constructively" with the board. He had survived the first major battle.

—

The board had sidestepped the issue, but Arthur S. and those allied with him remained determined to take control of the company.

The board took four significant actions the following month: (1) it hired an executive search firm, Spencer Stuart, which was seen as the first step toward replacing Arthur T.; (2) it approved a one-time $300 million payment of "excess cash" to shareholders, all of whom were members of the founding Demoulas family; (3) it established a credit facility, an indicator that Market Basket may have been looking to use debt to expand—something it had avoided doing while growing to seventy-two stores; and (4) it made it clear that they intended to replace two of the trustees of the company's $500 million profit-sharing fund. Only Arthur T. would be kept as one of the plan's three trustees.

"You don't hire a search firm, and they [the search firm] don't take the job, unless they're confident they're going to place a person," said retail consultant Neil Stern shortly after the August board meeting.

In an unusual move, the three independent (A/B) board members— Keith Cowan, Nabil El-Hage, and Ronald Weiner—sent a letter directly to associates days after the meeting. They tried to assure them that the board was making decisions "solely in the best interest of Market Basket," that the board had "no plans" to change the company's "more for your dollar" philosophy, and that it had "reaffirmed its commitment" to the employee profit-sharing program. The directors also thanked employees for their loyalty, dedication, and "strong and positive feelings toward Market Basket."

The letter went on to say, "We, like you, all want the best for Market Basket and are firmly committed to seeing Market Basket continue to thrive as New England's leading grocery chain."

The letter did little to appease associates. They shot back days later with a letter of their own. For the first time, intense feelings between associates loyal to their CEO and the board of directors who wanted him fired were out in the public. "Fear and anger . . . have now taken root in all of us," it said.

The letter, signed by hundreds of associates on a Facebook page, demanded to know why, given the company's success, directors appeared to be on track to replace Arthur T., who would replace him, and whether the profit-sharing program would continue. "We respectfully request that you show yourselves. Come out of the shadows and tell us who you are and why you are on board in what we believe to be the ruining of a great American company," the letter said. "If you believe we have been sold a bill of goods and that the facts will come out showing that we have been duped, then by all means, enlighten us."

—

That summer was the first time that associates had united so forcibly in response to what they believed was a threat to their company. It would not be the last.

A movement was born.

This group of committed associates did not realize it yet, but it was to be a practice run for the protest of 2014. The early protests provided a testing ground for new tactics, such as the use of social media as a communication and organization tool. It was a time in which associates discovered their voice, and managers gained confidence in their ability to confront board members directly. More than anything, it was preparation for a much larger battle than they could have ever envisioned.

9

"All In"

After the confrontation in July 2013, Arthur T. had managed, with the help of thousands of associates, to hold onto his job as CEO. But it was only temporary. The board held firm to its agenda of removing him and ratcheted up the pressure on Arthur T. and his team.

The board was more than just flexing its muscle; it was taking concrete steps to change the entire business model of the company. In essence, Market Basket was to look much more like its competitors. They wanted to replace Arthur T., they wished to disburse a huge sum of cash to shareholders immediately, they planned to take on debt for the first time, and they moved to change the way that Telemachus's prized profit-sharing plan functioned. It was an attack on all fronts.

That fall, two affidavits filed in court confirmed that Arthur S. had tried to find replacements for Arthur T. in June and July 2013. Joseph Rockwell, vice president of grocery sales and merchandising, said Arthur S. approached him at his house and asked if he would be interested in becoming a copresident of the company. Rockwell, now seventy-three years old, said he might consider it "if [he] was fifty years old" and said he was very happy with the way Arthur T. was running the company. Arthur S. then said the CEO would be removed at an upcoming board meeting and that he had long intended to take over operations of the company, according to the affidavit. Another manager, Jack Demoulas, the director of dairy and frozen food and a cousin of both Arthurs, said Arthur S. went to his house in June, saying he intended to fire Arthur T. and asked if Jack would be interested in becoming a co–vice president with Rockwell. Demoulas said he suggested something "less drastic."

The board moved the location of most subsequent meetings to Boston's Prudential Tower, home of the prestigious law firm Ropes & Gray. This was designed to prevent those loyal to Arthur T. from demonstrating as they had done at the Wyndham Hotel in Andover the month before. While people could not gather there en masse the day of a board meeting in September 2013, a select group of associates decided to quietly wait in the lobby to make their plea to directors as they entered the building. One person in that group was Scott Patenaude, who works as a meat manager in the Burlington, Massachusetts, store (#24). Not sure at what time the directors would show up, or through which entrance they would arrive, the group arrived early in the morning and waited and watched anxiously in all directions. Patenaude says he wanted to tell the directors that the path they were on would hurt a lot of people. When they did arrive, the B directors, Bill Shea and Terry Carleton, chosen by Arthur T. and his sisters, stopped to engage in some brief conversation. But he says that Arthur S. walked by, saying only, "I'm not answering any of your questions," and that Board Chairman and A/B Director Keith Cowan "didn't even break his stride." Patenaude and others interpreted this as arrogance by those directors. They recall feeling that their voices were being ignored as the board made decisions that could harm nearly everyone at their company.

It became obvious to senior managers that the board had a clear agenda, one that didn't include Arthur T. and probably involved selling the company. A number of senior managers began to prepare for the worst. One of these managers, Tom Trainor, recalls the conversations with his wife and kids early on. He, like many others, remembers thinking that the most likely outcome for supporting Arthur T. was that they would be fired themselves. But he recalls telling them, "This guy's been too good to us. He needs our help now."

All the while, the movement was growing and learning.

They rallied support where they could, hoping to forestall what began to seem inevitable. They found ways to communicate with associates outside of work. Trainor fell into the role of managing the protests' social media presence. In the subsequent months, the "Save Market Basket" Facebook account, which had been deactivated after the last meeting, was reactivated. A blog called We Are Market Basket was created to give access to those who did not have a Facebook account. That social media presence would become a key platform over which the movement's members communicated, shared ideas, and coordinated rallies and other actions.

Each time the board made a public announcement, Trainor and others would deride it in posts on Facebook and the blog site. Store directors and other members of the Market Basket family wrote "guest blogs" to convey the broad-based support.

In November 2013, some members of the board of directors, with the help of a public relations agency in New York, set up their own website at dsmboardinfo.com (the site is now defunct). It was an unusual tactic for a board to create its own website, circumventing its own CEO. The website stated that it was "intended to provide factual information from the board of directors about the company's corporate governance." Loyalists to Arthur T. believed the site had inaccuracies—in fact, Directors Shea and Carleton, as well as management, refused to endorse it. The site contained an unusual mix of content. For instance, on one page was an update on a store opening, while on another page was the rationale behind its vote to pay out $300 million to shareholders (the company "had accumulated cash far in excess of its needs as determined by management") and a prediction that profit margins would be smaller than those of the previous year. Arthur T. and other senior managers were outraged that the board would release information on the cash position and profit margin of a privately held company. The site also had a Frequently Asked Questions section. One question was whether Arthur T. would remain. "The Board is not currently looking for a new President," it stated. (The statement was later deleted.)

This irked Arthur T. loyalists, who knew that the board had voted to approve hiring an executive search firm the previous summer. To those loyalists, the statement suggested that the board was not being honest or forthcoming.

Some Arthur T. loyalists decided to undertake an e-mail campaign to the three independent board members. Patenaude was one of these loyalists. He says he doesn't know how many others, like him, began peppering the directors with questions, comments, and observations. Patenaude provided some of these e-mails, which include some sharp exchanges over the period of about a year. In one exchange with Ron Weiner, Patenaude raises concern about decisions by the board's compensation committee on which Weiner sat. "For someone as 'educated' as yourself, I expected something a little better. . . . Your compensation committee has a great effect on my ability to provide for my family. If it's more carpet baggers that fly in for a check, I think I have a right to know. In my opinion, you and this board can't see the trees through the forest."

Twenty minutes later, Weiner wrote back, "Dear Scott, Thank you for your thoughts. Once again you demonstrate your misinformed biased ignorance. By the way, the expression is 'Can't see the forest for the trees.' Bye."

In another exchange, Patenaude writes Weiner, "We are not going away" and "looking forward to the announcement you have resigned your position on the board. Have a great day." Weiner responded within six minutes, "Thanks for being the gratuitously obnoxious person you continue to be. Have a great day, Ron."

—

The battle spilled into the courts. Two decisions went against Arthur T. and the Market Basket movement. First, in September 2013, Suffolk Superior Court Judge Judith Fabricant denied a preliminary injunction request to block the disbursement of $300 million to shareholders. Then, in February 2014, Fabricant issued another ruling against Arthur T., who had sued to remove Board Chairman and A/B Director

Keith Cowan from the board and nullify his votes. Market Basket's bylaws required that A/B directors be "disinterested, independent directors." The suit claimed that as a former A director, Cowan was not disinterested and independent and had voted "under the controlling influence" of Arthur S. Demoulas. The judge decided that there wasn't enough evidence to send the case to the discovery phase, where emails, voice mails, financial records, and depositions might have been examined. Furthermore, her decision left little room for any form of rebuttal or appeal.

The ruling was a blow to the movement and enabled directors to continue—seemingly unfettered—with their push to remove Arthur T. as chief executive. For members of the growing movement of Arthur T. loyalists, the decision meant that the company would not be saved by the courts. To achieve their goal, they would have to take matters into their own hands.

—

As the summer of 2014 approached, associates were uneasy but united around Arthur T. A year had passed since the initial uprising of 2013, and his firing loomed over each board meeting. Nevertheless, on

"A/B" Directors	
(Independent) *Chairman:* Keith Cowan, Atlanta Ron Weiner, New York Eric Gebaide, New York	
"A" Directors	**"B" Directors**
(Aligned with Arthur S.)	(Aligned with Arthur T.)
Arthur S. Demoulas, Boston	Terry Carleton, Needham
Gerard Levins, Hopkinton	Bill Shea, North Andover

Market Basket Board at the Time of the 2014 Protests

June 23, 2014, Arthur T. prepared for a board meeting as if it were any other. Since before six o'clock that morning, Arthur T. had been busy preparing market share numbers to present to the board. Less than six hours later, he was no longer the CEO.

The board also fired two of Arthur T.'s top executives, Bill Marsden and Joe Rockwell. When news of the three terminations was received at headquarters, three associates immediately packed up their personal belongings and walked out. Four more did so the next day.

—

The board replaced Arthur T. with two co-CEOs. It was an unusual move, even for these unusual circumstances. During the past twenty-five years, only twenty-two Fortune 500 companies have tried to place two people at the helm. Most attempts have failed. However, both of the new CEOs brought years of industry experience.

Felicia Thornton, who was given the title of co-CEO and chief operating officer, last worked as the CEO of Knowledge Universe US. She's also served as a director on the board of Nordstrom and worked in executive roles for two large grocery chains: Albertsons and Kroger.

Jim Gooch was named co-CEO and the chief administrative officer. He was most recently president and CEO of RadioShack. He also held various roles for Kmart and Sears. More ominously, his former boss (when he was chief finance officer at RadioShack) was on the board of directors of Delhaize Group when Delhaize was rumored to be a pre-ferred bidder to buy the Arthur S. side's shares of Market Basket.

Thornton was to oversee all operations, including the stores; Gooch was to concentrate on finance and information technology. Both Thornton and Gooch served in consulting roles for Market Basket before being appointed to run the company. Both had contracts that guaranteed payment for three years, giving them a total salary that experts estimated would normally fall between $1 million and $3 million.

Market Basket is not a company that takes changes in personnel lightly. In fact, two offices at headquarters, which are considered the best by senior managers, have been vacant for years. No one has ever requested to move into either of those offices. The reason? One office belonged to Telemachus Demoulas until his death in 2003. The other belonged to Julien "Julie" Lacourse until his death in 2007. Both offices are "retired," just as hockey player Bobby Orr's number 4 is retired with the Boston Bruins or as basketball player Larry Bird's number 33 is with the Celtics. Associates see it as a sign of respect.

Given this penchant for tradition, it should come as no surprise that the experience of seeing two new CEOs enter the building was surreal. Most of the senior management team had *never* seen someone enter one of those offices who hadn't once pushed a cart in a Market Basket parking lot. Add to that the fact that these two were replacing a man who had become a symbol of everything that the company stood for, and it was more than most could swallow.

The new chief executives arrived in separate cars. They had no idea what to expect, so they brought a private security detail. They also walked in the door that first day with a group of computer specialists. Their entourage numbered close to a dozen in all. Trainor, Tom Gordon, and others watched in disbelief.

—

Tom Trainor says that even after months of warning signs, seeing the new CEOs enter the building still "felt like I got punched in the gut." He wanted to write a post on the We Are Market Basket blog but found it nearly impossible to put his feelings into words. "The well was empty," Trainor said. He wasn't the only one who felt the jolt. Phone calls buzzed back and forth all day between senior managers, store directors, and other associates. Many store directors offered to shut down their stores in a show of solidarity. Others advised that despite the store directors' noble intentions, such a move could create a civil liability. They might be able to be sued for losses. For the moment, the one thing they agreed upon was that they wanted Arthur T. back and that they needed coordinated action to do it.

The next two weeks were shrouded in uncertainty.

In those first days, the new CEOs kept a low profile. They met with top management and displayed a cool and calm demeanor. They were stepping into a minefield, and they did their best to move slowly and deliberately. Thornton began quietly approaching individuals to create a team of people who would report to her. Trainor and Tom Gordon were among these. She asked Trainor if he would be interested in a promotion to take on a bigger role in the company. He was stunned. He had just lost three of his greatest mentors and was being asked to take their jobs. It would be like moving into Telemachus's office. "No disrespect, but I'm not even sure if I can work for you yet, never mind taking on a bigger role," Trainor told her. He led another rally of more than a thousand people that afternoon outside the largest store in the chain in Chelsea, Massachusetts.

Surprisingly, Thornton and Gooch made no efforts to introduce themselves to anyone but their direct reports. For example, neither CEO visited any of the buyers who worked at headquarters. These employees are responsible for purchasing nearly 50 percent of items on Market Basket shelves. It could be that the CEOs shied away from speaking directly with subordinates because they were reticent to circumvent a chain of command, stepping on senior managers' toes in the process. But this hands-off approach was antithetical to the culture at Market Basket. Associates in the office interpreted their distance as the CEOs feeling superior to associates.

There were other missteps.

Throughout the next two weeks, the CEOs organized a series of meetings. They had a conference call with the store directors on Thursday, June 25. The CEOs spoke directly to store directors and assistant store directors only. They did not invite any of the senior management team at headquarters. (Some ended up listening in on the call at stores nearby; managers had invited them.) One store director asked the CEOs if there were any plans to fire any associates. Thornton and Gooch said there were not.

Firings had been on the minds of many in the room for more than a week. On June 16, days before Arthur T. was fired, Gerard Levins, a board member loyal to Arthur S., had arrived at Indian Ridge Country Club in order to install Sterling Golf Management to take over the club's operations. The club is owned by Market Basket, and relations were close between club staff and Market Basket associates. The change

Arthur T. Demoulas arrives at the Wyndham Hotel in Andover for a July 2013 meeting where he and his supporters feared he would be fired. It was the first meeting after control of the board of directors shifted from Arthur T. and his family to his cousin and rival, Arthur S. Demoulas.
Courtesy of Lowell Sun / Photographer David H. Brow

The eight managers at the forefront of the rally were, from the left, Dave McLean, Joe Garon, Dean Joyce, Joe Schmidt, Tom Gordon, Tom Trainor, Steve Paulenka, and Jim Lacourse. Combined, they had more than 260 years of experience with the company. McLean quit the day after Arthur T. Demoulas was fired. The rest were fired, along with Michael Kettenbach (not pictured), two days after the boycott began.
Courtesy of Lowell Sun / Photographer David H. Brow

Steve Paulenka, a manager who had been fired a day earlier, waves a stack of signatures of customers and employees demanding that Arthur T. Demoulas be reinstated as CEO. Courtesy of Lowell Sun */Photographer David H. Brow*

This rally, at the Stadium Plaza Market Basket in Tewksbury on July 21, was the first of a series held there in July and August.
Courtesy of Lowell Sun/*Photographer David H. Brow*

Photo by Daniel Korschun. When customers joined the fight to reinstate Arthur T. Demoulas, they went to many of Market Basket's biggest competitors, such as Hannaford, Stop & Shop, and Shaw's. Many returned to their Market Basket on their way home just to tape receipts, such as those above, to the doors as a sign of how they were willing to take their business elsewhere.

Photo by Daniel Korschun. Lawmakers quickly joined the side of Market Basket workers and customers, calling for Arthur T. Demoulas to be reinstated as what was in the best interest of the public. At the microphone is then State Senator Barry Finegold of Andover. To the right is Senator Sal DiDomenico of Everett and State Representative David Nangle of Lowell. Behind DiDomenico is Senator Eileen Donoghue of Lowell.

Photo by Grant Welker. Weeks into the boycott, Market Basket cut the hours of part-time store workers to match falling sales. But employees still stayed loyal to Arthur T. Demoulas, as seen in this photo at top right. Employees also had the support of customers, as is clear in the copy of a Lowell Sun newspaper advertisement at bottom left.

Photo by Daniel Korschun. When Market Basket vendors stopped delivering groceries in protest of Arthur T. Demoulas's firing, the first items to disappear were fresh produce, which were typically delivered every day.

Photo by Grant Welker. Empty shelves combined with existing signs, such as in the meat department of this Lowell Market Basket, provided a jarring image during the boycott.

Photo by Daniel Korschun. The Market Basket saga caught the attention of local media, such as WHDH Channel 7 in Boston, seen here in July 2014 at a rally in Tewksbury, Massachusetts, as well as several national media outlets.

Photo by Daniel Korschun. Protesters in front of the Hudson, New Hampshire, store. Rallies and protests held during the summer often included children.

Arthur T. Demoulas returns to Market Basket's Tewksbury headquarters the morning after he reached an agreement with competing shareholders to buy out the company. Here, he climbs onto the truck bed of Steve Paulenka, in the foreground, with a stuffed giraffe in the background—a symbol of the employee and customer movement.
Courtesy of Lowell Sun */Photographer David H. Brow*

would result in the firing of several managers at the club, its workers feared. First on the chopping block would be Cheri Nolan, the general manager of Indian Ridge who had worked there for forty-two years.

Levins arrived during a fundraising event accompanied by two representatives from Sterling and a small police detail. Nolan called 911 as well as senior managers at Market Basket. Those managers sent out a call on social media to gather at the country club. Hundreds of associates, mostly from Market Basket stores, rallied in the club's parking lot throughout the week. They said they were defending members of the Market Basket family.

The board and the new CEOs backed down. The next day, a statement that was issued read, "The Board apologizes to Cheri Nolan and all associates. Cheri Nolan and her management team remain in place at the Indian Ridge Country Club."

It was another victory for the growing movement of supporters. But emotions were still raw. "The uncertainty is an awful way to live," said Nolan.

More than anything, the confrontation left many with the feeling that the new chief executives could not be trusted. As one manager told us, "Artie [T.] has never lied to us. You might not always like the answer you get from him, but he's never lied to us. And here these people are [shortly after taking over as CEOs], and they're lying to us."

The CEOs missteps would continue throughout the protest. Weeks later, when many employees had walked out, the CEOs issued an ultimatum to workers to get back on the job. On July 30, the executives announced they would hold job fairs on three days the following week, posting available positions for store directors, accountants, and grocery buyers. "We need associates to return to work on Monday, August 4th," they announced. "We understand that some associates may choose not to return, consequently we will begin advertising for employment opportunities." Any worker that returned by that date wouldn't be penalized, they said.

Aug. 4 came and went without workers returning. In fact, there were more picketers at the job fair than applicants. Subsequent bluffs by the CEOs were similarly called by associates. "I don't work for them," said Rosie Vacirca, a grocery buyer of 20 years. "They can't fire me."

—

In the corporate offices, a deep unease crept in. "Those weeks [right after Arthur T. was fired] were the worst I have ever experienced working for Market Basket," says Linda Kulis, accounts receivable supervisor. Kulis is energetic and talkative by nature, but during this period, she says she was at a loss for what to do. She had a strong loyalty to Arthur T. and other company leaders. She remembers Bill Marsden making the rounds at the office the day he was fired, trying to say good-bye to as many people as possible. He was apologizing for having to cut good-byes short; if he had stayed in the building much longer, it would have been considered trespassing.

Beyond the loyalty, staff did not trust the motives of the new CEOs. Each had histories at large companies that bore little resemblance to Market Basket. But more important, no matter which way staff in corporate looked at it, the facts always added up to an eventual sale of the company. Those who had been around long enough (and in the office that has most staff) had seen what happened to Maine-based Hannaford when it was taken over by Delhaize; much of the corporate function was consolidated and moved to North Carolina.

Barbara Paquette, accounts payable supervisor, sums up her feelings, "They weren't here for our best interests." She, like so many others, is deeply embedded in Market Basket. Her husband, father, and other family members all work at Market Basket. Her future, on so many fronts, depended on Market Basket remaining healthy and in Tewksbury. "There was a lot to lose," she says.

Making matters worse, the new CEOs never introduced themselves to Paquette, Kulis, or others. The unfortunate visual image that remains for many is that of Thornton and Gooch entering the building with bodyguards.

—

The next week, Thornton and Gooch called a management meeting. Arthur T. had earmarked bonuses for the senior management team based on another year of strong performance. The new CEOs were no doubt pleased to be able to deliver these checks themselves. Normally this meeting was held in a large conference room at the Indian Ridge Country Club, but fearing that this would irk managers, they chose to hold the meeting in a small room at the distribution center at headquarters. However, the room could only fit about half the people they needed. They decided to split the meeting in half, inviting a few people to attend both meetings to convince associates that the CEOs were giving a consistent message to all managers.

At the first meeting, Thornton spoke for five minutes, then Gooch for five minutes, before opening to questions. The second meeting used the same format, but Gooch spoke first, Thornton second. They hoped for a dialog to clear the air.

Market Basket associates are very outspoken, but the culture is not to confront leadership in large, public meetings. Questions and challenges to supervisors tend to come during one-on-one conversations or in small group meetings. This meeting was different. Attendees peppered Thornton and Gooch with questions about their conversations with the board of directors and their personal motivations.

One question was, "Have you been involved in, or do you have any knowledge of the company being put up for sale?" Thornton and Gooch sidestepped the question, saying, "That's a shareholder decision." When pressed if they had knowledge, Gooch said he did not.

Another question put to the CEOs was, "You [Thornton] are from Oregon, and you [Gooch] are from Minnesota. Do you have any plans to move your family here?" Both Thornton and Gooch were noncommittal. She said that it would be some time before she could decide about moving to New England because she had one son in college and the other in boarding school. Gooch offered that his wife was going to be in Massachusetts for a visit that weekend.

After the meeting, the impression of many in the room was that the CEOs were withholding something. In a culture that values honesty and integrity as much as Market Basket, this was viewed not only as a breach of trust but also as a sign of weakness. Furthermore, the answers fueled speculation that they were installed in order to facilitate a sale, not to lead the company over the long term.

—

An informal group of eight senior managers began to meet at five o'clock each morning. They discussed how to send the board a message and how to wrestle back control of the company. At first, they met in the offices. Sometime later, they moved these discussions to a more secluded place outside. They chose a corner next to a dumpster outside the office. It was fitting for a group of senior managers who prided themselves on being willing to get their hands dirty. In a lighter moment, one joked that they were "the dumpster eight."

The plan was straightforward. They would make a simple demand: bring back Arthur T., along with others who had been fired. If this demand was not accepted, they planned to shut down the company. They calculated that the most effective way to shut it down was not to close the stores but rather to disrupt supplies from the warehouse. That would hurt sales while simultaneously maintaining the costs of operating stores. It also impacted seven hundred warehouse employees rather than all twenty-five thousand in the workforce. But they needed broad-based support among all associates.

They called a meeting at headquarters. They assembled the full corporate office staff in the lunchroom and laid out their plan. If the CEOs fired one manager, everyone would walk. They asked for support and offered anyone who was not in agreement the chance to leave.

Then with everyone still assembled in the lunchroom, they brought down Thornton and Gooch. They gave the CEOs their demands. Thornton and Gooch were to go to the board and request that Arthur T. be returned with full authority. They wouldn't work for anyone else. There was to be no discussion. The group had agreed beforehand on a code word to end the meeting; when the group had finished laying out their demands, Tom Trainor said the code word. Everyone stood up in unison and began to file past a stunned Thornton and Gooch. "They were just standing there with their mouths open," recalls Trainor.

—

Nine long days passed. The group continued to rally support and plan for the worst, but there was still silence from the CEOs. On July 16, a few senior managers visited Thornton in her office. They reminded her of their demands and gave her a deadline of 4:30 P.M. the next day. They said that if they received no answer, they would consider it a no. As they turned to walk out, Thornton lost her cool for the first time. "You've got your answer in the *Boston Globe* today," she shouted. Sure enough, an article in the *Globe* restated the board's support for the new CEOs.

The next day, Trainor, Tom Gordon, and Joe Schmidt each received conciliatory calls from Thornton. She asked each of them if they would like to speak with the board by phone on the following Monday. She reiterated her desire to work with them. She was hoping to restore some continuity to a management structure that was fragmenting before her eyes.

But at 2:30 that same afternoon, Thornton and Gooch sent a companywide e-mail threatening to replace anyone who walked off the job. The curt e-mail began by stating that the CEOs had asked the board to convene a special meeting to discuss demands from associates. Then they addressed each associate in an appeal to their self-interest:

> We believe that while all the communication to us has been represented as unanimous—this is an individual decision that each of you has to make, whether you wish to continue to work at Market Basket. To be clear—doing your job is continuing to do the same type of work that you regularly do every day—not newly defined tasks from your supervisor. If you choose to abandon your job or refuse to perform your job requirements, *you will leave us no choice but to permanently replace you* (emphasis added).

Senior management and associates were livid. "They were threatening everybody in this company with termination and replacement like they are a piece of furniture," says Trainor today.

By now, the full senior management team was at headquarters. They called everyone down to the lunchroom again. Rather than striking fear in associates, the e-mail seemed to have galvanized them. According to Trainor, the consensus at the meeting was, "They are not going to meet our demands; we are walking out of here at 4:30 today, and we are not coming back."

At that point, Thornton and Gooch, who had no doubt sensed something was afoot, entered the room. A shouting match began. Associates barked questions at the CEOs. The CEOs tried to defend themselves and also struck back with accusations and orders of their own. The situation had completely unraveled for these two seasoned veterans. They were in disbelief. With little more he could add, Gooch began shouting, "Just go to work. Just go to work."

At 4:30, a small contingent of the press greeted staff and senior management leaving the building. Barbara Paquette's eyes still well up thinking about it. Her husband, father, brother, and cousins all work at Market Basket, so she had "a lot on the line" and a lot of history. When it comes to her career, Market Basket is all that she and her family know. She gathered some personal photographs and made her way to the front door with her colleagues. She says she remembers it like it was yesterday—"walking down those stairs, not knowing if we were coming back."

"This isn't work for all of us; this is a family," Tom Gordon said. It was a group that was clearly unnerved and anxious but also determined. "You take down one, you get the twenty-five thousand behind us," Gordon said.

Steve Paulenka added, "We're a crazy bunch. If this was a poker game, we just went *all in*."

—

That Sunday, Thornton and Gooch made it official. They sent couriers to the homes of eight corporate employees: Joe Garon, Tom Gordon, Dean Joyce, Mike Kettenbach, Jim Lacourse, Steve Paulenka, Joe Schmidt, and Tom Trainor. Each received written notification that they were fired, effective immediately.

10

"Shut It Down"

The day Arthur T. was fired and replaced with Felicia Thornton and James Gooch, Dean Joyce called his warehouse staff together in his break room. Joyce is the supervisor of the early shift, one of two daily. Although trouble had been brewing for a year, Joyce was caught off guard as much as everyone else. His "guys" knew something was wrong by the look on his face. Just about everyone, about two hundred altogether, had worked with him for years, and they knew he wasn't the kind of person who buckles under the day-to-day pressure of moving products. It must be something serious. Joyce gave them the news straight.

"They just fired Mr. D."

There was dead silence.

"I don't know about you, but I'm not going to work for anybody else but Mr. Demoulas. If they're not going to fix this thing, we're going to have to do something. I hope you guys are with me."

By the time Joyce stepped foot into that meeting, he had already contemplated walking out. His workers had the same visceral reaction. Many wanted to walk out then and there. They knew how important they were to the company's operations and what a message it would send if they quit or went on strike. But Joyce had come to an agreement with other members of the senior management team that it would be better to wait and form a more thoughtful game plan. The warehouse staff thought it over as well. They were on board.

The time to take action came a few weeks later. On Thursday, July 17, senior managers in the corporate office cleared their desks to leave at the end of the day. Joyce spoke to Bill Mackey who oversees the second shift, which ends at 1 A.M. on Friday mornings.

"I'm walking out today. All of my guys are on board. How about your guys?"

"We're good, we're good."

Joyce remembers second-guessing himself about whether he was making the right call for his group. "Geez," he asked himself, "Will Mr. Demoulas like the fact that we just shut the warehouse down?" He could think of no other way.

—

If Market Basket were a human body, the warehouse would be the heart. It pumps the lifeblood of products into the stores. It beats to the rhythm of shoppers' purchases. When demand is steady, the warehouse hums regularly, and when demand spikes, say around the Christmas season, the Warehouse beats faster to accommodate. Each store opening puts additional pressure on the warehouse to pump more and more.

Entering the warehouse at Market Basket is a bit like entering a hidden world. Clues to the bustle inside can be seen by the dozens of trucks waiting to drop off or pick up. But it is still difficult to comprehend that this single building in Tewksbury is supplying more than seventy stores with most of the grocery products that will appear on their shelves (another warehouse in Andover supplies perishables).

The physical space of the warehouse is massive at five hundred thousand square feet, with a ceiling about thirty feet high. The space is too large to walk quickly, so almost all workers use golf carts and other electric vehicles to get around. This gives it a feel of traveling in a city with no traffic lights. Vehicles of different shapes and sizes are driving in all directions, beeping horns before turning corners around full pallets stacked six to ten feet high.

Garage doors, which trucks back into, line the warehouse walls except on the side attached to the corporate offices. These doors are the same size as the back doors of an eighteen-wheel truck. It isn't obvious that trucks are even there; one sees a series of deep tunnels formed by the insides of the trailers. Along the far back end—the south wall of the building—are the doors for deliveries. Manufacturers, such as Proctor & Gamble, drop off pallets of Tide, Gain, and their other branded products here. These pallets are unloaded and moved to giant shelves of inventory; products are stacked neatly all the way up to the ceiling. One group of employees is dedicated to receiving and placing these pallets into inventory.

When the warehouse receives an order from a store, the selection process begins. Selectors go to the shelves and grab the amount of the product that the particular store needs: one hundred boxes of Colgate toothpaste, fifty boxes of Market Basket brand oatmeal. Then selectors pack forty-inch-by-forty-eight-inch pallets to fit perfectly into the truck without leaving extra space. Readers who have played the video game Tetris may appreciate how these pallets are crafted by selectors. It is equal parts art, science, and good fortune. The pallets are lined up next to trucks at the doors on the west side of the warehouse. Once twelve full pallets are created, the shipment is loaded and ready to travel to the store. They do this more than 100 times per day, and on some days, they hit 150.

The goal of the warehouse is to fill each order accurately and quickly without ever sending out a truck that is not 100 percent filled to capacity. The warehouse needs to stay in constant communication with both stores and buyers in the corporate offices, since their role is to efficiently and effectively connect the manufacturers that Market Basket buys from and the stores that Market Basket sells from.

The warehouse is physically attached to the corporate offices. To visit those offices, one has to drive through the same lanes as tractor-trailers. Drivers can be seen milling outside. There is a palpable feeling that the office is closely linked to those warehouse operations. There is a nearly continual flow of salespeople visiting buyers, and each of those buyers can literally see their products, and those of competitors, driving by in the white Market Basket trucks with the big "more for your dollar" logo on the side.

It takes a certain kind of person to work in the warehouse. "The warehouse guys" are known as a rough-and-tumble bunch. They are disciplined, but during breaks and the rare down time, there is a hint of a locker room vibe in the air. They sometimes push the limits and have been known to hurl plastic containers at each other in the aisles. Mostly they enjoy throwing friendly jabs back and forth or making the case for their favorite sports team.

A number of workers grew up in the New York area, so the historic Boston–New York rivalry is a source of lively debate. One of their favorite stories is of worker Mike Holland entering the warehouse the day after the Red Sox came back from a 3–0 series deficit in the 2003 playoffs to beat the Yankees in seven games. He was wearing a full Red Sox uniform: cap, top, pants, and official socks. Throughout the day, before and after work and during breaks, he ran around the warehouse waving a whiffle ball bat as a victory dance. "Even the Yankees fans couldn't help but laugh," remembers Joyce.

—

The day of the warehouse walkout, Dean Joyce's brother Scott, who works as a truck driver for Market Basket, turned to Dean to reassure him. He told him that they were going to win and that he shouldn't be too worried because the current CEOs and their staff didn't know anything about Market Basket. He joked, "They don't even know where to turn on the lights."

The first warehouse shift, the one that Dean Joyce oversees, ended at 3 P.M. As they handed the reins to Bill Mackey's group on the second shift, it started to sink in that the next day, they wouldn't be working inside the building as usual. They would be showing up for work, but to picket.

When the second shift finished at 1 A.M., Joyce entered the warehouse to close up as he often did. He set the alarm. He shut off all the lights and turned off the circuit breakers. A few hours later, a small crew arrived. It was composed of around twenty warehouse workers who decided to cross the picket line and a small number of contract workers brought in by the CEOs; they had been expecting a walkout. When this group opened the doors at around 5 A.M., they tripped the alarm.

It was the unofficial announcement of the warehouse walkout.

Steve Paulenka arrived at the site in the early hours of the morning. By then, the alarms had already sounded and could be heard from quite a distance. "That's the first time in thirty years I heard those alarms going off," he said. "They were pretty loud." They would continue to blare from the warehouse for hours as replacement workers tried to figure out how to disable them.

Joyce arrived an hour later. He also heard the alarm. As he drove by the back to assess things, he noticed that the lights were still out. They still hadn't found the circuit breaker board. He chuckled to himself, "Scott was right. They really don't know how to turn on the lights!"

Senior managers had walked out the day before, but it would be a few more days before Joyce and the other fired managers would become persona non grata, barred from entering the premises. He entered his office to take home some personal items. As he walked out, he bumped into one of the replacement workers and told him that those in the replacement staff were in over their heads. He was doubtful that any outsider could successfully operate the Market Basket system. "They just didn't know how we run our show," he said. "You may have [experience] somewhere else, but we're a different animal here."

Joyce was largely right. Deliveries from the warehouse slowed to a near standstill. The first day, nothing went out at all. In fact, replacement workers spent much of the first day looking for keys to the trucks. They had been placed neatly in an unlocked box in Dean Joyce's office.

The following week the warehouse sent out fewer than ten trucks per day. Even after a few weeks, many trucks were filled only to a fraction of their capacity. Joyce found out later that they received orders for 250 thousand cases; "That's nothing for us; we'll bang that right out" in a day, he said. It took the replacement crew weeks to fulfill an order of that size. They had neither the knowledge of Market Basket's processes nor the manpower to do it.

Associates in the office say that trucks were sent to the Claremont, New Hampshire, store, one hundred miles away, carrying a single pallet of water. They say that on a trip like that, with such a small load, the goods would arrive damaged.

By the end of the protest, Joyce had gotten to know members of the Tewksbury Police Department quite well. They were placed on detail at the picket line daily. Those officers claimed that Market Basket protesters were the best-behaved picketers they had ever seen. In fact, there was only one reported incident during the protest. It involved a replacement driver who, frustrated by taunting from picketers, jumped out of his truck during a delivery and threatened protesters with a hammer. The man was arrested.

—

One of the workers in the warehouse was Luis G. Mendez. Mendez immigrated to the United States from the Dominican Republic during his teenage years. His first jobs in the United States were in construction in Boston. Those jobs paid the bills, but he says they cannot compare with his current job with Market Basket. He's been with the company for nine years and plans to stay many more. He relies on the generous benefits and bonuses to care for his family; he is married with five kids (the oldest is thirteen years old and the youngest eight months old). But just as important, Mendez likes working at Market Basket because he feels close to his colleagues and to his supervisors.

Mendez remembers returning home after his last shift before the walkout. He told his wife Margaret that he had walked out.

"We gonna stay strong, and we gonna be with Dean [Joyce] outside. Whatever happens is gonna happen to everybody."

"Are you sure? Are you comfortable with this?"

"Yeah, I can't cross the line. I need to be there for my company, for everybody."

"All right. Whatever you have to do, you do it. If I have to work overtime in my job, I'll do it."

For the next six weeks, Mendez took care of the kids on Saturdays, the day that his wife took an extra shift at the cleaners where she worked. To make ends meet, the couple relied on her extra income, their savings, and two checks from a fund that protesters had started to supplement the income of striking warehouse workers. Even so, his family was stretched. He says he is still paying down some credit card debts he acquired during the protest.

Mendez says those six weeks felt like a year. "It was a scary time." He came in every day at 7 A.M. to "fight for the company" until about 2 P.M. Mendez and others treated it like a full-time job without pay.

Meanwhile his family, in-laws, and friends all offered their opinions about what Mendez needed to do. Even his mother pressed him: "If you are going to do this, make sure it's not because you feel pressured but because it's what you think is right." He assured her that this was his decision and only his.

A couple of his closest friends jumped the line. When they did, his friendships with them ended. He says they stopped speaking to him. Those colleagues still work at Market Basket but have kept their distance. Mendez says he doesn't understand it; he appears to hold no hard feelings, but the tension and sadness is evident in his voice as he looks back to lost friendships.

—

After working at Market Basket for five years, David Courteau, the grandson of a French-Canadian who immigrated to work in a factory, found the climate in the warehouse to be better than other places he's worked. He says that in other jobs, he'd feel like "the low man on the totem pole" with marginal respect and not much hope for advancement. At Market Basket, Courteau says that everyone is treated equally. It is a climate, he says, that "starts with Arthur T." and the kind of environment where if "you work hard, they notice it."

He says that Market Basket's benefits and bonuses have helped him and his wife of two years make progress toward paying off her student loans. Nevertheless, money was already tight, and the walkout put even more stress on their finances. Courteau normally took care of the mortgage payments on their house, while she took care of other bills.

Courteau remembers returning home after his shift on Friday and seeing Steve Paulenka and Tom Gordon on the news moments after they had walked out. He says earlier that day, warehouse workers had met as a team, and each person was asked to decide whether to strike or cross the line.

He told his wife he had to walk out because it was something he believed in. He felt that if they didn't stand up now, there might not be a Market Basket anyway. "You sacrifice six weeks out of your life for your future, it's well worth it." He says it never even occurred to him to cross the picket line. He also stresses that protestors weren't "asking for more money, or better benefits, or anything for [themselves]. [They] just wanted to bring the guy back that was in charge."

Both of his parents supported his decision. Other family members were more skeptical. He says that some wondered aloud why he would enter a fight they said was really between two billionaires. But Courteau didn't see it that way. "It was bigger than that; it was more the people in here," he says. "If you don't work [at Market Basket], then it's hard to explain how it is, how we are together." He says that from the first day, "I knew I was on the right side [of the picket line], and I had faith it was going to work out."

After a few weeks, it became clear to Courteau that he wasn't going to be able to pay his bills that month. He received two checks from the warehouse fund, which he used to buy food and other staples. But he worried about how he would pay some of his creditors. He started calling them to see if something could be worked out. The national creditors were not terribly helpful, but local creditors obliged. One was the company that performs the maintenance on his townhouse and another was the Service Credit Union. Employees he talked to at the credit union "were fans of Market Basket" and worked with him to create a payment schedule that would do the least harm to his credit score.

These were difficult times for Courteau and his wife, but he says it was worth the sacrifice. "It was amazing seeing that many people stick together," and it "was one of the best things I did in my life."

—

At one of the rallies, Dean Joyce spoke about the impact that the warehouse had on the protest. "I'm so proud of [the warehouse workers], because you can see that when they're not around, there's nothing happening at these stores. The shelves are empty. They are realizing now what I've been saying for years. You guys are the best in the world."

But closing the warehouse operations was not enough for the movement to take flight. There was still a chance that stores could continue to operate normally. Those seventy-one locations had to follow suit.

11

"Stick Your Neck Out"

It was sunny and seventy-five degrees. August 16, 2014, was a beautiful day for the 115th Old Home Day Parade in Londonderry, New Hampshire. Ten thousand spectators lined Mammoth Road for this annual New England tradition. Marching was an eclectic mix of politicians, local businesses, youth groups, motorcycle clubs, church leaders, marching bands, and bag pipers. They received applause from the crowd as they moved past the main stage.

As the parade was nearing a close, a large contingent of marchers appeared in the distance. Faint cheers of "Artie T.! Artie T.!" could be heard. They were coming from 130 full- and part-time Market Basket associates, more than a quarter of everyone employed at the Londonderry store. Most wore matching navy blue t-shirts, which read, "We believe in ATD [Arthur T. Demoulas]" on the front; the back was designed like a football jersey with Londonderry across the top—where a player's name would appear—and a large number forty-two (the number of the store) below it.

The contingent was led by an associate in a giraffe costume, the assumed mascot of the Market Basket movement. It had become so when Gordon LeBlanc, spoke about it at a rally early in the protest. He says the LeBlanc family uses it as its mascot because it reminds them, "Do not be afraid to stick your neck out when you know you're right." After that speech, giraffe cartoons and stuffed animals began popping up at Market Basket rallies and picket lines.

By the time the emcee introduced "the employees of the Londonderry Market Basket," the crowd had already risen to their feet for a standing ovation. The cheering was by far the most spontaneous, loudest, and longest of the parade. Some people stepped into the street to give the associates high fives of encouragement. Store director Mark Lemieux recalls that "people came up to [him] afterwards to say, 'you guys rocked the parade!'"

For Lemieux, the ovation was thrilling. He had talked to individual customers and heard people honking their car horns in support as they drove by associates who picketed outside the store. But he hadn't known what to expect at the parade and was surprised at the intensity of support from this community.

The event was also moving for another reason. When the town invited Market Basket to participate in the parade, Lemieux knew he had to ask for volunteers. Many of those volunteers would be people he had been forced to lay off just days before. It was a lot to ask. The number of people who participated and the response of the crowd that day rekindled his faith in the protest. "It was the most emotional thing I've ever been to," he says.

—

Store associates became a visible force during the protest and ensuing customer boycott, but some had been finding ways to support Arthur T. for more than a year. One of these people is Cindy Whelan, the store director of the Market Basket in Epping, New Hampshire (#63), which lies about midway between Portsmouth and Manchester. A twenty-six-year veteran at Market Basket, she's been with the company since she was seventeen years old and is married to a former Market Basket associate (he left his job to take care of their children).

She began her campaign early. About nine months before the summer protest of 2014, Whelan joined many other store directors in writing e-mails to the board of directors. In part, she wanted to open a dialog in which she could learn "their side of the story." But she also wanted to educate the board that the situation was much more complex than they might have appreciated. She says that the board was myopic; they seemed to think that changes to the company would only affect senior management and associates. "I wanted them to understand that it's not just the associates, it's the customers, it's the communities, it's the fire departments, it's the schools," she said. "If you mess with Market Basket, all these people are part of that."

For example, her Epping store is one of only three establishments in that city that employ more than 250 people (close to 500 people work at the store). She has very close relationships with local organizations like the local police department. She relies on them for any shoplifting issues, and they rely on her. A week before our interview with Whelan, a couple of police officers dropped by her office—after eating lunch in the Market Basket café—to update her on some youth programs they were running and to ask for her support in doing fundraising. When in May 2014, police officer Steve Arkell was shot and killed on duty in the nearby town of Brentwood, Market Basket supplied water and food during the vigils.

When Whelan sent e-mails making her case to the board, some board members, such as El-Hage, responded very professionally. But she says that the reaction of one of the independent A/B directors surprised her. He first replied to one of her e-mails in October 2013. Whelan was pleased to be able to have a direct conversation with a board member. The first e-mail was professional and constructive. They began to exchange e-mails every now and then. She wondered why this board member continued an exchange with her but not other store directors; she knew others who had written just as many e-mails to the same board members. But she was just happy to have someone's ear on the board. It evolved into a conversation over many months up until Arthur T.'s firing.

As time went on, she says the e-mails became increasingly "defensive" and at times "condescending." She says that as a store director taking issue with a board member, the insults and finger pointing in the e-mails she received "got pretty scary for [her]." Despite these fears, she continued to press. The board member would disengage for periods of a month or so, only to return with another blistering message. Once Arthur T. was fired, all communications from the board stopped.

—

In the earliest weeks after Arthur T. was fired—but before senior managers walked off the job—associates would take their breaks near the entrance to the store in a show of support. They stood with signs. They set up tables to collect signatures. Inside stores, signs in support of Arthur T. began to pop up across departments. Glass panes behind the deli counter, which would normally announce specials of the week, carried messages such as "ATD is our CEO." During this period, sales were still brisk, but associates were busy telling customers that the business model of their favorite grocery was in jeopardy.

By July 20, eight more senior managers were fired, and the warehouse had essentially shut down deliveries. Inventory dwindled quickly. Perishable foods disappeared first. Meats were gone within days. Signs for the "best meats sold anywhere" and "fresh poultry delivered daily" hung above empty bins. In the produce department, only yams, ginger, and a few other vegetables remained after a couple of weeks. In the shelf area, where onions and apples normally lay, some associates arranged empty cartons to spell out "ATD." Dairy continued to stock some fresh milk, but only the bare minimum, and little of this was sold.

The middle aisles were sparse. By their usual standards, the shelves were a mess. Associates normally say that a meticulous aisle should have the look of a smooth wall—items arranged to meet the edge of the shelf. Now nearly every aisle had gaping holes. Clerks continued to tidy up what remained, but even this work was initiated more out of boredom than urgency.

This left stores with an odd mix of foods. For example, no fresh fruit was available, but dessert shells for strawberry shortcake and packaged fruit dip (with an expiration date of nearly a year later) remained. The Merrimack Valley Food Bank was a short-term beneficiary of those empty aisles. Market Basket sent it nearly two thousand pounds of bread and rolls, along with other produce. The donation was large enough that the food bank canceled its weekly bread order from a commercial bakery.

Roaming the empty aisles could be eerie. Some would visit simply to experience such quiet in a store normally teeming with shoppers and workers. "It's an introvert's paradise," said Tucker Martin, an eighteen-year-old who was wandering the empty aisles of Lowell's Bridge Street store with three friends around 5:30 P.M. on a Tuesday. "It's like Chernobyl," his brother Andy said. Tucker shot back, "except instead of radiation, there's no food."

—

With the warehouse strike putting a stranglehold on deliveries, store associates fought to keep stores empty of both products and customers. It began in what supermarket people refer to as "the back of the store."

During normal times, the Londonderry store receives many dozens of deliveries per day. Some are from the Market Basket warehouse, but just as many are from local vendors. It is a consistent train of deliveries. Their store warehouse is designed accordingly. One of the chain's largest, it can comfortably fit ten to fifteen full truckloads of product. The refrigerated section in the back of the store is large enough to bring in pallets with a forklift.

Sean Morse, an assistant store director in Londonderry, says that during the protest of 2014, deliveries dropped to a couple per week at most. As he gave a tour of their impressive facility, he described periodic skirmishes that erupted at the loading docks and in the parking lot. "We had some pretty good battles back here," he says. The altercations never turned violent, but they were very heated. "They tried to deliver a load; we'd refuse it," Morse says.

It was replacement drivers who delivered to Market Basket during the protest. Many of these were professionals—condottieri working on a contract basis for a private company specializing in crossing picket lines. They placed security in the parking lots during deliveries and sent in teams to videotape deliveries to intimidate strikers and discourage resistance.

The most effective tactic at stores was to refuse shipments for not conforming to Massachusetts and New Hampshire state regulations. Many replacement workers came from out of state and were not familiar with these regulations, so stores used their knowledge to turn away products. To prevent tampering between loading and delivery, trucks are sealed with a multidigit code. Stores are sent the code by the warehouse, and if the code does not match, they know a load has been tampered with at some point after loading. During the protest, when a truck arrived with a perishable load from a refrigerated truck without a seal, stores would turn it away. Even when deliveries did conform, store associates would try to slow down the delivery enough that the driver would not be able to make deliveries to other stores. This led to long debates. It was a battle of wits.

In one altercation, the store had parked a white trailer in the way of deliveries. Emblazoned above the Market Basket logo in large red letters was the word "BOYCOTT." Employees surrounded the trailer with their own cars so that no one could move it without illegally touching the cars. Even after a visit from police, the delivery did not go through.

In the end, stores were able to refuse about a third of deliveries and delay the rest enough to "put sand in the gears," as one store director put it. The deliveries they did receive were grocery loads that were weeks late. To put this in perspective, stores usually place orders two days before they need something; an order might be placed on Wednesday for delivery on Friday.

—

At the front of the store, associates asked customers to boycott Market Basket until Arthur T. was back in charge.

While associates encouraged customers to shop elsewhere, most retained their feeling that Market Basket played an important role in the community. At no time was low-income families' reliance on Market Basket for affordable groceries more evident than during the protests. Most customers boycotted the chain, but the protest put some others in a bind. These customers *wanted* to support the growing movement. However, they weren't sure if they could afford to do so. It was simply too expensive to take their business to one of Market Basket's competitors.

Associates understood how important Market Basket was to these people. While they offered directions to the nearest competitor to those who asked, there was no evidence that any associate ever heckled customers who continued shopping there. They knew some people had no choice and viewed Market Basket almost as a form of public service to these customers.

"You have people who can't afford to go anywhere else," a manager of the Wood Street store in Lowell said.

Jane Raposo, a Lowell resident and mother in a low-income household said, "I feel bad this is all happening, but I can't afford to go anywhere else." Another shopper, Rita Parks, was in a similar predicament. "I support what they're trying to do," she said about a week and a half after the boycott began. But with her limited income, Parks said she had little choice but to continue shopping there. She apologized to employees at the Wood Street store in Lowell for what she called "crossing picket lines."

This was a fairly common occurrence. "They come in almost apologetically," said Dave Delaney, the assistant director of the Fletcher Street store in Lowell.

—

Store directors were isolated from the corporate offices. With most senior management gone, having either walked out or been fired, official channels to the corporate office were severed. Store directors who, under normal circumstances, would call Tom Gordon, Jim Lacourse, or other senior managers, were left to get the ear of two CEOs: Thornton and Gooch. Managers called and wrote e-mails to the CEOs. Overwhelmed, the CEOs responded to e-mails en masse, sending one or two per week to all store directors.

Ironically, these store directors were updated quite frequently by senior managers who were no longer working in the corporate offices. They saw them most days during the week when they picketed together outside the Tewksbury warehouse. Then they would see them again on the weekend at the stores. Senior managers like Steve Paulenka would spend the weekend on the road, visiting more than a dozen stores per day. They used those visits to cheer on part-timers picketing curbside and to inform store directors of new developments.

It was as if there were two Market Baskets. The official Market Basket was being run almost entirely by outsiders. New CEOs sat nearly alone in the corporate office with a team of newly minted information technology employees. Replacement drivers drove near empty trucks from the warehouse to stores, only to come back with the same load some of the time.

Meanwhile, the unofficial Market Basket was chugging along seemingly effortlessly. It was a strikingly unified group, this shadow organization that identified itself as We Are Market Basket. And it was a group that the new CEOs and the board of directors seemed ill equipped to rattle. Store associates were fiercely protective of their supermarket and others in what they considered the Market Basket family. And they felt that their family was under attack. Walking through the crowd at the rallies or visiting the picket lines outside of stores, the sense of a unified group was unmistakable. They held signs reading, "Arthur T. is OUR CEO." They hugged associates from other stores, some of whom they had just met.

Some people questioned whether a nonunion workforce could sustain a protest over weeks. But their sense of unity, based on their affiliation with the company, was as powerful as any union membership. "This company never needed, or ever will need, a union," Operations Supervisor Joe Schmidt told public radio station, WBUR. "We're far stronger than that."

At one point at a rally, early on, Gordon Leblanc, a meat supervisor and buyer, approached the podium. Steve Paulenka introduced him with a certain nervousness in his voice. He said, "Now our next speaker knows there are children in the crowd. I've warned him to keep it clean." It was tongue in cheek; he had to have had an inkling of what would come next. Leblanc is known to be brash and has a tendency to use rough language, especially when he is passionate about something.

About a year prior to this rally, Red Sox star David Ortiz spoke at a pregame ceremony to mark the first game at Fenway Park since the marathon bombing that had rocked Boston. He famously said, "This is our fucking city and nobody's gonna dictate our freedom."

Leblanc ended his impassioned speech with the same allusions to group unity. He was not going to let anyone tell him who was in charge. He growled into the microphone, "This is *our* fucking company!"

—

Associates leaned on other family members for support. Karla Foster says many mornings, she would wake up and ask herself, "Is this a nightmare?" Foster fought for Arthur T. and the company, but she also fought because she worried for her son, Phillip. He has long-term special needs and Market Basket's plan covered those needs. "Where else would I get that?" she says thankfully. But Foster was concerned that a takeover by another company could change her health insurance benefits. "He would have lost his doctor because she doesn't take Medicaid," she says. "I wasn't sure that's what was going to happen, but it wasn't a chance that I was willing to take."

As the days dragged into weeks, the protest became more and more trying. Even picketing on the street, usually an uplifting experience as passersby honked, could sometimes go sour. Infrequently, someone would pass by and yell insults from his or her car window: "Go back to work!" some associates heard. There were many days in which Foster and others felt defeated, saying things like, "I can't do this anymore."

But then Foster says she would have a meeting with Store Director Mark Lemieux and renew her resolve. "He deserves a lot of credit," she says, "because he held us together." He called meetings daily, even on his vacation days, to motivate his staff. According to Foster, he never said, "*If* we win." Instead he always said, "We're gonna fight for this man, we're gonna win, and Artie is not gonna let us down." She says that if Lemieux was scared or nervous, he never showed it.

Foster was mostly right. Lemieux was completely committed to the movement, but he was not invulnerable to his own doubts. He has not worked for another company since he started as a bagger for Market Basket almost four decades ago. "Everything I have is because of this company and the Demoulas family," he says. Lemieux has been with the company for thirty-seven years, which just so happens to coincide with the number of years he has known his wife. If you are wondering how that could be, it's because they met at store #2 in Lowell during his job training.

Lemieux had faith in the outcome: "I was all in. I didn't have a plan B. I didn't look for another job." But he also had "dark days," days in which he looked for motivation from his Market Basket family members. He spoke to people like Foster, who lifted his spirits. He went down to the road to picket and hear cars honking in support "to pick up that energy again." He spent days in the hot sun at the corporate offices in Tewksbury bringing water and food to warehouse workers who were without pay for almost two months; "to hear the warehouse people thanking us," he says, "that's what kept us going."

Lemieux still gets emotional describing the sacrifice that many of his associates made to contribute to the movement. "I'm proud of my people," he says, holding back tears. "I'm not a cocky man, but yes, yes, I'm very proud to say it: this store led the charge."

He begins to list the many associates who found their own role in the protest. Barbara Broome is one of these. She has worked in the deli department for ten years. Lemieux says she was one of the part-time employees whose hours he was forced to cut: "I had to tell her she can't work anymore, and she has bills like we all do. She pays the same for gas, and milk, and bread just like we all do. To tell her you can't work and then for her to come every day—she would go by the road every day in the belief that it was the right thing to do."

He tells also of Sue Mawson, who he describes as being "a breath away from losing her home." Nonetheless, she was at every rally. Some days Lemieux would arrive early in the morning in Tewksbury (an hour's drive), expecting to be the first one there; Mawson would already be picketing.

—

The culture of empowerment that pervades Market Basket in good times paid off in difficult times. Store associates took whatever role they thought would help the cause.

The Epping store needed vehicles to get to the Tewksbury rallies, which were an hour away by car. An associate called the local branch of the national bus rental company First Student and persuaded them to donate busses for the day. They packed those busses with dozens of associates and customers, sending them to the rallies.

An associate at the same Epping store started an ice bucket challenge to raise money for warehouse workers who were without a paycheck. Cindy Whelan and assistant store directors were among those who had some very cold, very wet moments. The challenge spread to other stores as well.

Associates ordered t-shirts and sold them at cost to fellow associates. They purchased posters, markers, and other supplies. They organized trips to the corporate office.

—

Speaking to store directors, there was one moment that they consistently refer to as the most difficult of their careers. Cindy Whelan, the store director in Epping, New Hampshire, we met earlier, says she got the news while she was in the store about four weeks into the protest. It came from the corporate office, a notice from the CEOs. All store directors were to eliminate the hours of part-time associates. Stores were hemorrhaging money, and store directors were to get personnel costs in line with sales within the next pay period.

"It's almost like sabotage," said Whelan, whose store employs 450 workers, 40 of whom are full time. "It's impossible." The Epping store needed to meet a payroll threshold of $177 in sales per man-hour worked, she said. At that standard, she said, it "wouldn't even cover salaried [department] managers."

Whelan gathered herself and called a meeting in the front aisle of the store; the store was empty, of course. She looked around at the thirty or so part-timers in the group. One of them was the daughter of one of her best friends, a store director in Rochester. There were mothers. There were retirees who supplemented their social security with their paycheck from Market Basket. "I broke down in tears," she says. After weeks of trying to protect them from just such an occurrence, she says, "I felt like I failed, that I let them all down."

Many workers took the news to mean they were laid off, which the company had to insist later in the day was not true. "I have issued an immediate communication for all store directors. All store directors are to let their associates know that they are not laid off," Thornton said in a statement e-mailed by the company. "All store directors as part of their normal responsibilities are able to and often do reduce hours but they need to make clear when doing so that the individuals are still employees of (Demoulas Super Markets)." The clarification was a response to pressure by Massachusetts Attorney General Martha Coakley, who had warned the CEOs that her office was watching the events closely.

"I feel like the directive (from Market Basket executives) is a setup to fire the store directors who've done nothing wrong," said Steve Zaharoolis, a front-end manager at the Wood Street store. Other managers felt the same way. "Now they have a reason to fire us," Lemieux said. "Sales are down, you're not making payroll."

"This is the toughest thing we've ever dealt with," said Lemieux. "They're the backbone of our company, this part-time work force. The doors are open, we're open for business, but the customers are completely boycotting the stores. It's an impossible task."

According to store directors, overnight, staffing at most stores was reduced to a skeleton crew—15 percent of its normal levels. Only full-time employees and department heads were left.

The last remaining hope for store directors was that the cut in hours—for all intents and purposes, layoffs—would serve as a wake-up call to the public that if Market Basket were to reach the point of insolvency, the region would have to deal with a very grave situation.

It did catch the public interest. Customers in particular showed their loyalty through the protest.

In the final two weeks of the standoff, Felicia Thornton sent a stern message to store directors to clear items blocking loading docks and remove all nonessential signs—that is, anything related to the boycotts, Arthur T., or the Warehouse and Truck Driver Fund. Associates responded by calling for additional signage. "As of for the Fund, let's make sure that buckets are at all entrances," read a message from the We Are Market Basket blog site.

12

"Market Basket Strong"

The warehouse had shut down supplies, and stores had stuck their necks out in solidarity. But the new CEOs, Felicia Thornton and Jim Gooch, figured that if they could garner enough customer demand, they could outlast the protesters and eventually replace associates who remained loyal to Arthur T. and his management team. That would get the company running and ready for a sale again.

What they had not counted on was the loyalty of Market Basket customers. "As soon as we asked people to stop coming in, it pretty much stopped," Foster said.

Many companies have loyal customers. What made this situation unique was the proportion of customers who were loyal and the nature of that loyalty. Market Basket provides an egalitarian experience, one that fosters unparalleled loyalty. Interestingly, the motivations differed somewhat for customers compared to employees, but many customers were motivated by a sense of purpose, felt like they were a part of the Market Basket family, and relied on a resourcefulness all their own.

As senior manager Joe Schmidt said, "It's in the customer's hands right now."

—

Similar to employees, customers felt a sense of purpose when they supported the protest. However, they sometimes saw a different meaning than employees did. While associates cited the direct impact that Market Basket has in their communities, customers placed the conflict in even larger terms. They viewed this as a sort of David and Goliath struggle—one that pitted workers against the forces of corporate greed.

James Post, the Boston University professor, says that many protesters "wanted to give a vote of endorsement to the things that Market Basket stands for." Even those who had not shopped at Market Basket in the past were inspired by this purpose. He says a lot of people interviewed on the picket line said things like, "You know, I haven't been a big Market Basket customer, but I really love what they are doing, and I want to be a part of that."

Jack Christian had been a customer for many years. He doesn't know employees by name, but he does recognize many familiar faces each time he enters the store. Christian has been a prominent member of the plumber's union for almost fifty years and feels empathy for the cause of employees. He was thrilled to see employees organize in disobedience to the board of directors: "I could see these people doing the same thing that we have talked about doing forever, you know? If things are not going right, stand behind your guy. They just believed in this guy enough to say, 'You know, let's lose some paychecks; we don't care. He took care of us in the past, and he will take care of us again.' More power to them."

For Christian, associates were contributing to a long-running struggle. He could probably see parallels between the Market Basket protest and past strikes, like the Bread and Roses strike in Lawrence a hundred years prior. He was motivated to join the movement to continue this struggle.

People like Susan Nolan, a longtime customer, also saw a larger purpose to what customers were supporting through their boycott. She was worried about what lay in store for workers at Market Basket and how that might affect the economy as well. "It wasn't even about the prices. This was so emotional for me. I'm choking up as I'm telling you that." Nolan says that she's too often read about corporate greed over the past decade or more. "I'm a hospice chaplain; I have a soft sweetheart side but not when I see people being used and abused." For her, the board of directors was abusing Market Basket associates. "[Arthur T.] didn't do that. He isn't an angel, but he's an angel to them." Each time she drove past Market Basket to visit a competitor's store, she felt she was contributing to a greater good.

Rita Stone concurs. She has been a Market Basket customer for as long as she can remember. Her mother shopped there when she was a child. She remembers the rides that were present outside the supermarket doors; as a child, they were the highlight of any grocery trip. She shops almost exclusively at Market Basket now. Her son used to work there too as a part-time bagger and carriage mover.

She describes the company as a "well-oiled machine" with hardworking associates. "I mean they have several people in there that just go, go, go."

The protest renewed her appreciation of Market Basket. She says, "Most people didn't realize how good they had it until they thought that they might not have it anymore." She did not hesitate to join the protest by boycotting the store.

She worked across the street from a Market Basket store and was impressed with protesters' dedication. Associates were a constant presence outside the store. Every morning on her way to work, she'd honk her car horn as she passed by. Thousands of others did too. "When you see this every single day, it literally put a lump in my throat." She remembers that the associates were "willing to lose their job to stand up for what they believe is right, which is totally unheard of, and quite inspiring."

And Stone recalls that her boycott changed how and what she ate. She got some of her produce from her neighbors, who operate a farm. What they couldn't supply, she would travel to New Hampshire for. She thought it "made no sense [that] if we're going against 'corporate greed,' we're going to go to Stop & Shop or Wal-Mart." In her eyes, defecting to a large corporate chain would be counterproductive because she would be giving her money to another company that prioritized shareholders above employees and customers. She made an exception for some of the gluten-free items she needed, which she bought at Trader Joe's (owned by a German trust that also operates the Aldi chain).

Stone did not stay out of Market Basket stores completely, though. She made occasional visits to salute the associates who worked there. She wanted to let them know that they had her support. "Good job, guys!" she'd say. She also donated money to some of the funds that were popping up. One of these was in support of warehouse workers who were still striking.

Social pressure from other customers in the Market Basket family was intense. Stone recalls that some people would say that they were tired of the boycott and that they were thinking about purchasing a product there that they couldn't get elsewhere. "People will tell them, you can't go in. You can't go to Market Basket. They'd just say, 'No!' It wasn't allowed. It just wasn't."

Stone observed what many others did. Customers pressured other customers to boycott even more than associates did. Associates would encourage people to boycott, but never was there a report of heckling a customer who entered a store. Associates assumed that shoppers had no alternative. "It was a positive protest," she says. She tells a story to drive this point home:

Right at the very beginning of this strike, when I first heard about it, I went over there. One of the guys in the Deli—I can't remember his name. I see him all the time. My son worked with him when he worked there, so he's worked there for quite a long time. We always chit-chat a little bit. I said, "I'm going to be totally honest with you. I know that I'm not going to be able to have brown-sugared ham for a while." It's Market Basket's brown-sugared ham. I love it. "Here is the thing," he said. This is on the first day or something. "We need to clear out the store too," he said. "Once everything is gone, we have nothing to sell because nothing else is coming in. If you buy a pound or two of brown-sugared ham, you're helping us empty the shelves." He said, "I'll be more than happy to get you some brown-sugared ham." He got me some brown-sugared ham, and I think it was the last thing I bought until the end of the strike. When it ended, that was actually one of the first things I got when I went over there. He was one of the first people I saw, too, going into the store.

Not surprisingly, the young man in the deli remembered that Stone wanted the brown-sugared ham.

—

The sense of family at Market Basket unified not just employees but also customers. During the protests, customers acted on that feeling, providing remarkable support as they joined the movement.

Nowhere was customers' support more evident than in the August 2 and August 3 editions of the *Lowell Sun*. Those days, a full-page advertisement appeared on the back page of the front section—a coveted placement for advertisers. It was directed at the board of directors and the new CEOs. The ad was designed, written, and paid for by customers who decided that they needed to make a public statement of their support for Arthur T. and the protest in general.

It was a group of people scattered across Massachusetts and New Hampshire with no affiliation to the company other than having purchased their groceries at Market Basket for years. One of these people was Jaymie Stuart Wolfe, a writer and editor living in Wakefield, Massachusetts. She had been following the protest on Facebook and the We Are Market Basket blog and wanted to do something to help. She says she already had "an activist streak" in her and wanted to see this succeed. She had seen other protests become derailed after just a few people made unconstructive statements out of anger. She would wake up some mornings, and the first thing she would do was post a short, inspirational quote on the "Save Market Basket" Facebook page. She figured that might set a tone that would help keep the online forums positive. She noticed that she wasn't the only one doing this.

The customer ad was created in response to one taken out a few weeks prior by the new Market Basket executives. New CEOs Thornton and Gooch had placed an advertisement in the *Boston Globe* two days after senior managers, corporate office staff, and warehouse workers walked out. They were advised by the New York public relations firm Kekst and Company. It appeared in simple black and white on a full page (page A5) and was titled "An Open Letter to Our Customers and Communities." It began, "We want you to know that despite any differences that may exist amongst members of the Market Basket's founding family, we all agree that you, our customers and the communities we serve, come first." The CEOs went on to praise customers and those associates, saying that they "had the opportunity to see firsthand many of the traits that make Market Basket so beloved." Then the ad went on the offensive, lashing out at those who were picketing across the street from headquarters. "This has been an emotional time for many associates," it read. "Unfortunately . . . some have lost sight of the top priority—taking care of you."

The message raised the ire of many customers. Those customers had built a rapport with associates over years, and they didn't like the new CEOs equating supporting Arthur T. with turning on customers. In fact, many customers saw it as the reverse.

An idea surfaced on social media that customers should take out their own ad. Wolfe saw this and was one of a handful of people who thought this might be her opportunity to play a constructive role. She began to follow this discussion closely, contributing ideas when she could. Another customer organized a fund-raiser through the website gofundme.com. In a matter of days, they raised more than $20 thousand—much more then they needed to purchase the ad. (They donated the remainder to a fund to support the warehouse staff who had gone without pay for six weeks.) They decided to place the ad in the *Sun*. The group felt that it was important to go with the *Sun* "for historical reasons." Not only was the company founded in Lowell, but the *Sun* also seemed to reflect the unassuming values of Market Basket.

A version of the ad was floated on social media. Wolfe liked the ideas in the proposed ad but thought it was too verbose. She thought she could improve it, strengthening its message. In her spare time—she works full time at Pauline Books and Media in Boston—she put together a version of her own and posted it. It gained support right away. It read,

> To the Current CEOs of Demoulas Market Basket,
> Board of Directors, and Shareholders:
> A full boycott does not depend on Associates:
> It depends on CUSTOMERS.
> It is YOUR CUSTOMERS who are boycotting your stores.
> It is YOUR CUSTOMERS who bring in the money.
> It is YOUR CUSTOMERS who are your bottom line.
> It is YOUR CUSTOMERS who will not shop at
> Market Basket until Artie T. is back as CEO.
> It is YOUR CUSTOMERS who paid for this ad.
> #YouCantFireCustomersWeQuit

Wolfe says she had two main goals as she crafted the copy. First, she wanted to make it clear that this message was from customers. The idea was to show the board, the replacement CEOs, and majority shareholders that unless they brought back Arthur T., they would have to contend with two million customers. This is evident in the second line of the ad. The second goal was to communicate resolve. She wanted readers to be left with no doubt that customers were committed to the boycott. We see this especially in the final three lines of the ad copy: "will not shop," "it is YOUR CUSTOMERS who paid for this ad," and "#YouCantFireCustomersWeQuit."

When the ad ran, it caused an immediate sensation. It went viral on social media. But it was also picked up by traditional media channels.

—

Associates displayed remarkable resourcefulness throughout the protests; as the customer ad demonstrates, individual customers found a role and then looked for unconventional ways to make progress. As the movement grew, others looked for innovative ways to join in support.

David Greenberg is a marketing director for a music booking agency and a Market Basket customer who shops in the Gloucester and Danvers, Massachusetts, stores. He says Market Basket has an ideal combination of product selection, prices, and service. Greenberg started making ginger beer last summer, and he finds fresh ginger at Market Basket at a price that allows him to buy it in large quantities. As many others observe, Market Basket's produce section has such constant turnover that fruits and vegetables are fresher than at many other supermarkets, and the aisles "are packed with many different things." And while at Shaw's or Stop & Shop, only three or four registers may be open, at Market Basket, "there's twenty lines, and they are all open. And they have stuffers, so the lines are long, but they go really quick," says Greenberg.

Greenberg knew little of the long running dispute between the two sides of the Demoulas family (respective heirs of Telemachus and George). But he remembers seeing statements by the new co-CEOs, Thornton and Gooch, when the protests began. He says he recognized the language they used. He had heard it before from CEOs at other companies that are more concerned with profits than people; they didn't "regard either [the associate] or the customer as integral to the company." He believed that the board and the new CEOs were probably "ensconced in their meeting rooms . . . or wherever the hell they were" and, thus, were out of touch with the needs and desires of customers. They couldn't and didn't understand his loyalty to Market Basket.

Greenberg got angry enough to take action. He decided to start a customer petition. His goal was to create a physical manifestation of customer loyalty that he could deliver to the corporate offices. If he could print out the names of a few thousand people, the new CEOs might be forced to confront the fact that customers loved the Market Basket business model. He had no illusions that this would turn the tide on its own, but he felt a need to add the customer's voice to this conversation.

MoveOn.org is a website designed to enable precisely this sort of petition. It claims to have a community of eight million strong. It started as a single online petition during Bill Clinton's presidency in 1998. That original petition collected the signatures of people who were tired of the Clinton impeachment hearings and wanted to "censure President Clinton and move on to pressing issues facing the nation." MoveOn has a liberal leaning and helped organize those wishing to end the war in Iraq, pass health care reform, and fight for economic fairness, according to its website.

As a grassroots movement fighting against what Greenberg and others saw as corporate greed, MoveOn seemed a natural place to start a petition. It was easy to set up and had a number of success stories.

It was important to Greenberg that the petition be *by* customers and *for* customers. While he did not bar anyone from signing, he stated explicitly that it represented the voice of customers, not associates and certainly not onlookers from other parts of the country.

It began with just a few online signatures. Then he watched it tick up at a moderate pace over the next couple of days. When it hit around two hundred signatures, those who ran MoveOn took an interest. They had read about the protest in the national news, and now that the online petition was gaining some traction, they offered additional support. When they contacted Greenberg, he explained that his goal was to print this out to deliver to the board and the new CEOs. MoveOn offered to pay for the printing costs and featured the Market Basket petition on its front page. MoveOn also discussed creating publicity by funding some advertisements on Facebook and other social media sites. MoveOn e-mailed all petition signers who were residents of Massachusetts and New Hampshire.

Suddenly, the numbers started to grow. The number of petition signatures was in the thousands now. Greenberg decided to send thank you e-mails through MoveOn. MoveOn does not provide e-mail addresses for those who sign the petition, but it does allow the administrator of a petition, Greenberg in this case, to send an e-mail to all those who have signed the petition to date. He composed an e-mail thanking signers for their support and asking them to pass along a link to the petition to friends and family.

Meanwhile, Greenberg monitored the "Save Market Basket" Facebook page to see what people were saying about the protest. To his surprise, he started seeing his name pop up in posts: "Who is this David Greenberg?" There was suspicion that the petition could be a ploy by the new CEOs to identify associates sympathetic to the protest and fire them. Greenberg found himself explaining his motivations all over social media to allay fears.

Signatures did not slow down until the petition hit twenty thousand signatures. At this point, Greenberg knew he had enough to make some sort of impact. He printed the full list of signatures. It required a few reams of paper and was 2,171 pages and five inches tall. He took pictures and began to send them to as many people as possible. He e-mailed photos to board members (he had found e-mail addresses for some board members on various websites). He contacted scholars who had been interviewed about the protest in the news. He e-mailed the print and television media. Fox News took some interest, but Greenberg pulled away when he saw the station run a story that customers were shopping at Market Basket despite the boycott. It didn't fit with his goals.

We will never know if any board member ever saw the photos of the printout (if so, it likely would have had a halting effect). However, Greenberg's determination to act on behalf of associates is notable as an example of a customer who contributed in the best way he could think of.

—

Many customers were not satisfied with simply boycotting. They wanted to contribute in other ways. These customers found unconventional and inventive ways of providing their support.

When some customers needed to do their weekly shopping, they would pass by Market Basket first to honk their car horn at picketing associates who were constant fixtures along the streets outside stores. The customers would drive down to the nearest Hannaford, Shaw's, or another market and fill their shopping cart. As they did so, they may have paid $200 instead of the usual $150 or $170 at Market Basket. They wouldn't drive straight home though. They would drive into the Market Basket parking lot, walk up to the front doors, and affix to them the receipt from their last purchase. Once the practice caught on, receipts could be found at most Market Basket stores. The receipts, measuring between six inches and two feet long had an almost festive look to them—like a series of white streamers decorating the entrance. More often than not, the receipts hung next to a poster of Arthur T.

Customer support reached social media in creative ways as well. Market Basket–themed songs hit YouTube, and even a fake, satirical Twitter account pretending to belong to the chain's board of directors popped up. Instead of the company's tagline, "more for your dollar," the fake Twitter account's tagline read, "more yachts for your dollar." Another fake Twitter account pretended to belong to co-CEO Jim Gooch. Someone also registered a website with the name of the other co-CEO, Felicia Thornton, for use as a page for supporting Market Basket employees. According to a message posted on Feliciathornton.com, it was meant for "entertainment purposes only."

Twitter hashtags like "#SaveMarketBasket," "#MarketBasketStrong," and "#ShutItDown" were popular, and customers posted photos to Twitter and Facebook showing empty produce shelves, empty parking lots, and rallying supporters of Arthur T.

Still other customers provided welcome breaks from long hours under the sun in the form of sweet treats. On one of the hottest days of the protest, the owner of Richie's Italian Ice visited picketers in Tewksbury. "They came with two vending boxes. That was the best day because it was ninety something [degrees]. . . . We were like, 'I love you,'" refrigeration worker Diane Patterson reminisces. "It didn't just happen in Tewksbury; it happened in every community," says Linda Kulis, accounts receivable supervisor. Patterson adds, "for the full six weeks too."

—

As Steve Paulenka said at one point during the protest, "The customers are the locomotive pulling this whole thing right now. They have shut this company down and they are not coming back until we come back and we are not coming back until our boss comes back."

13

"The Final Straw"

Once the Market Basket management team walked off the job, relationships between Market Basket and its vendors changed. With the corporate office mostly empty, official channels disappeared overnight. Orders dried up and so did checks.

Vendors that relied heavily on Market Basket were also badly hurting. Among those most affected was Phoenix Foods, which provides some of Market Basket's groceries and private-label items, like household goods, paper products, cereal, and pasta.

"They were the ones who stayed loyal to us, the local guys," said John Magliano, who founded the distributor. "We haven't had an order in about five weeks," said his son, Jim Magliano, who helps run the business. "We are essentially out of business until they're back in business."

Many farms across the Merrimack Valley saw their business drop badly. Riverside Farm in Methuen, which normally ships twenty thousand mums to Market Basket stores across the area in the late summer, was left unsure of where its goods would go.

"It's affected us greatly," said owner John Simone, who once worked for the grocery chain himself. "When you take losses in this business, there's no room for error anymore. The profit margins are so tight that when you take a hit like this, you're not going to make it up."

Pleasant Valley Gardens in Methuen was also left scrambling for other buyers. For thirty years, the farm sold Market Basket vegetables during the summer, mums in late summer and fall, and flowers for Easter in the spring.

It found buyers for summer squash, zucchini, lettuce, and other vegetables but at lower prices than Market Basket had agreed on, founder Rich Bonanno said. Whole Foods helped by buying fifty thousand of the eighty thousand mums it grew, but also at a lesser price.

"Just as we were getting into the peak of our season with our squashes, we were unable to move any product," Bonanno said. The century-old farm had been able to get by with enough income, he said, despite relying on Market Basket for two-thirds of its business. Bonanno, president of the Massachusetts Farm Bureau Federation, knew how critical Market Basket's orders were to small farmers across the area.

"One of the things they did well was they made an effort to buy as much locally grown product as they could," he said. "So when this happened, it wasn't hurting a California grower who maybe sold to twenty grocers. You're talking about businesses around here, and Market Basket is a big enough player that they're really hurt."

The Market Basket standoff also affected at least a few towns in New Hampshire that sell special pay-as-you-throw trash bags in Market Basket stores. Towns like Newmarket were not fully reimbursed for trash bags for weeks. "They always paid real quick," Newmarket Town Administrator Steve Fournier said. "As soon as we issued the bill, it was back within eleven to fourteen days. Then all of a sudden, it was a month, and we knew something was going on."

While vendors felt the pinch, a number of them sacrificed willingly. The shadow organization of fired senior managers encouraged vendors to halt or at least slow shipments until the protest ended. Many vendors felt a loyalty to those senior managers, which had formed over years and sometimes generations. Each vendor dealt with the conflict in its own way: some were vocal proponents for Arthur T., while others found quieter roles.

—

Tim Malley is the CEO of Boston Sword and Tuna and was perhaps the most vocal vendor during the 2014 protest.

Malley's company supplies swordfish, tuna, lobster, and other seafood to Market Basket and other supermarket chains. A thirty-year commercial fishing veteran, he has seen the best and worst of his industry over the years. He describes the seafood business as a "rough and tumble" one, but he tries to run a company that is professional and cares for suppliers, employees, and customers. He says a key to his success is the fact that his team marries these people skills with a deep knowledge of the seafood industry and information-technology savvy.

Malley and his partner, Michael Scola, built a strong relationship with Market Basket over the years, beginning when a competitor lost the account in 2007. Market Basket buyers came to visit the facility but were tight lipped about their intentions. Malley and Scola were proud of their state-of-the-art facility but couldn't tell whether they had impressed Market Basket. Within a week, the orders started coming in. The first orders came in for swordfish and tuna. Because these items come in so many different grades and sizes, they are among the trickiest wild seafood items to price. After a few successes, the account grew quickly. Within a few years, they were also selling scallops and salmon to more than fifty stores. Boston Sword and Tuna is now one of Market Basket's top seafood suppliers.

Meanwhile, one of BST's first accounts, Hannaford, which had been based in Portland, Maine, was purchased by Delhaize Group. They had been staffed by very knowledgeable buyers, but Delhaize moved seafood procurement to North Carolina without moving the talented managers they had in Maine. With the change, they "became increasingly more of the sharpen-your-pencil philosophy and less about quality," Malley says. As time wore on, he felt pressured to meet their price point at the expense of a good product. "It's just a very unconstructive way of doing business," he says. "We weren't happy with it."

When they started working with Market Basket, he found it a "breath of fresh air." Although Market Basket has low prices for consumers, "they made it quite clear from the start that they were not a cheap retailer," he says. Market Basket buyers knew fish, and they were local, so they were easy to build a strong relationship with. Overall, they found them to be much faster at making decisions and more accessible than most other retailers. They also liked the company on a personal level, and Scola would

attend Boston Bruins games with Bob Hartman and other Market Basket associates. During those outings, they would get to know each other's
families. The bonds became stronger and stronger. That personal relationship made it easier to trust one another when faced with the inevitable
ups and downs of the wild seafood business. Scola handled pricing and
would always do his best to meet a price point that Market Basket would
advertise, and Market Basket would ease price pressure on, say, salmon if
it realized it had gotten too aggressive on tuna the week before. It was "a
great working relationship" of give-and-take, and both were winning.

Like other vendors, Malley had followed the tensions between
Arthur T. and the board controlled by Arthur S. for more than a year.
When Arthur T. was replaced by Felicia Thornton and James Gooch
in the summer of 2014, he became extremely concerned for the well-
being of the fired management team and for the respective companies.
Malley felt an "obligation to do anything [he] could."

Malley and Scola were initially concerned because their company
wasn't receiving a payment of $700 thousand it was owed. This was out
of the ordinary because Market Basket was among his most respon-
sive customers and had always paid promptly. Inquiries seemed to be
going into a black hole, phones at the corporate office were not being
answered, and messages were not being returned.

Frustrated, Scola drove to Market Basket headquarters. He went
through lines of chanting and booing associates to get to the front door.
With an invoice in hand, he told a security guard that he was there to
see Felicia Thornton. Thornton accommodated him, sending him off
with a handwritten check for $400 thousand. Presumably, he gripped it
tightly as he walked by the jeering protesters.

The late payment took pressure off Malley, but what happened next
really concerned him. In the later weeks of the protest, they received
multiple *over*payments. The first overpayment was $83 thousand. Scola
and Malley ripped the signature off and mailed it to Thornton to show
that it had been voided.

Despite promises from Thornton that a new perishables manager
had been hired, no new orders came. Soon after, they received a call

from a new hire (who had joined from Albertsons, where Thornton had previously worked) who said that he expected to order seventy-one cases of each seafood item that Boston Sword and Tuna normally provided. They also sent a check. Once again, it was an overpayment. But this time, it was for $415 thousand.

To Malley, that was "the final straw."

Malley feared the possibility was that this was a deliberate attempt by Arthur S. "to sabotage the future of the company," that "the Arthur S. side of the family [might] be so embittered by the defiance of Arthur T. and all the stakeholders supporting him that their plan is to sell him—at full pre-conflict price—a pile of smoking rubble." The overpayments were consistent with the idea that Arthur S.'s side hoped to drain the company's bank accounts to make it more difficult for the company to recover from the conflict once Arthur T. took control again.

Of course, Malley did not know for certain what led to the overpayments. But he reasoned that whether the cause was malevolence or simply mismanagement, he needed to bring the events to light. He wrote an open letter titled "Letter from a Longtime and Loyal Business Partner" in which he stated the reasons why he and his partner had decided to dissolve all their business ties to Market Basket as long as it was under the control of Thornton and Gooch. He says that "it was the right thing to do" and that his partner, Scola, agreed, saying, "We gotta do something."

Malley was aware that he was placing himself and his business on the line. Friends and family were concerned. Some warned him, "I hope you know what you're doing. It could blow up in your face." They worried that he could be inviting a lawsuit. He stuck to the facts and tried not to make his accusations personal. He didn't want to fan the flames, but he did want to get the attention of lawmakers and minority shareholders and alert them to the fact that things were a lot worse than they probably imagined.

He posted the letter on his website and sent it to the *Boston Globe*, which published excerpts. The letter was also posted on the We Are Market Basket blog page, where it garnered more than seven thousand responses within days. Other newspapers picked up the story as well. It was part of the wave that turned the tide of the protest.

Looking back on his public statement for Arthur T. and the senior management team, Malley doesn't regret a thing. He says, "It was a high point for me in a career of forty to forty-five years."

—

Michael Fairbrother is the CEO of Moonlight Meadery, a vendor supplying honey wines to Market Basket. Meaderies like Fairbrother's have resurrected an age-old process of fermenting sugars from honey to produce barrel-aged wines, sparkling wines, and "melomels," which are made with fruit tones.

A resurgence of interest in these sweet wines has enabled him to expand both nationally and internationally. After twenty years in business, he sells in thirty US states and has buyers as far away as Australia. He is currently in negotiations with importers in China.

Fairbrother, a former Market Basket worker, considers the company to be one of his most valued customers—a strategic partner. State law precludes him from selling to Massachusetts stores, so his company supplies Market Basket across New Hampshire.

He admires Market Basket's negotiation skills. He warns others not to be fooled by the down-to-earth demeanor of Market Basket personnel. Don't plan "to do with business with Market Basket and think you are going to be dealing with amateurs," he says. He worked on a joint program once, in which he lowered the price of one of his brands for a month, and Market Basket passed the savings on to customers. It was great exposure for Moonlight Meadery, and sales volume was strong. Market Basket also stocked up on the brand during the sale and had inventory remaining, even after the sale was over. It provided an additional profit margin for a short time afterward. Fairbrother says this system ends up benefitting everybody: "We get a big bump in sales, they get a little more cash from our product," and customers benefit from the sale. He says that he has to remind himself now and then that if he "show[s] a little bit of skin, they may come after it." But he attributes Market Basket's negotiation style to smart business practices and suggests that this keeps him on his toes.

Market Basket is a high-volume buyer, but what makes his partnership with the supermarket strategic is the history of his relationship with the company. He credits Market Basket with helping him grow from from "essentially traveling at farmers markets to having [his] first commercial successful chain."

Other retailers claimed to support local vendors, but when Fairbrother approached these chains in the early years, they would not give him the time of day. In contrast, Market Basket was remarkably open. His early meetings were with Julien Lacourse, the man whose office remains vacant out of respect. "If you can come in and support your product by doing tastings," Lacourse told Fairbrother, "We are willing to give you a shot." He wanted Fairbrother to commit to Market Basket as well.

About six months later, Fairbrother had shown a very successful track record. Moonlight Meadery began to expand. He says, "They changed my life, and they are still changing my life." Fairbrother credits Market Basket not only with buying his product but also with making him a better businessperson. He remembers once, as he was hoping to expand from a single store to multiple Market Basket stores. After a miscommunication, he and his wife wrote to buyers. He says, in hindsight, the mistake was his own, but at the time, he thought that Market Basket was in the wrong.

Fairbrother says that buyers at other retailers might have ignored him or simply severed the exchange relationship. But he received a call from Julien Lacourse's son Jim, who coincidentally was one of the eight senior managers who was fired during the 2014 protest. "Michael, come on down," said Jim. "Let us straighten this up and try to figure this out because the tone in this e-mail seems a little off-putting." It was a show of respect and professionalism that impressed Fairbrother deeply. By the time he left the meeting with Lacourse, he understood what the miscommunication was and how to correct it. More important, he understood that he needed to emulate that professionalism in order to be successful at serving a large company like Market Basket. "We had to learn how to work in their culture, which is you set appointments, you set expectations you have, you have goals." Of the experience, "That really built that loyalty and trust that I have with them."

Over the years, Moonlight Meadery and Market Basket's relationship has blossomed. Fairbrother had to make some adjustments along the way. For example, his company's slogan is "romance by the glass," and the names of his more than three dozen wines, including "Embrace," "Fling," and "Paramour," can be suggestive. When Market Basket balked on his "Desire" brand, he created a less racy brand called "Blissful." It has been this give-and-take over the years that has deepened the relationship between the two companies.

During the year of the protest, from the summer of 2013 until June of 2014, Fairbrother received updates on the tensions each time he received orders and when he visited stores for tastings. As soon as Arthur T. was fired, buyers and store directors informed him that they planned to shut down the company.

Fairbrother didn't hesitate. He told his staff to stop calling Market Basket and to stop delivering Moonlight wines. "We are going to sit this off on the sideline," he told them. This was not easy for him. He says he feared for the future. Losing Market Basket as a customer forever "would have put me out of business," he says.

"For me, it was just loyalty," he says. Does he consider himself part of the extended Market Basket family? "Absolutely," he says. He maintains a close relationship with local associates and corporate buyers. Market Basket associates visit him frequently at his winery.

Like so many others in the region, Fairbrother had worked for a brief time as a teenager at Market Basket—one of his first jobs at fifteen years old. He still remembers Arthur S. Demoulas "driving through the parking lot in this Porsche 911 with a fishtail in the back." Meanwhile, "Arthur T. Demoulas was the guy coming in, and he worked," Fairbrother recalls. "He was a by-the-book type of person."

When the protest finally ended, Fairbrother visited the local store for the first time in many weeks. The store director greeted him warmly. "I want to give you a hug, but I will take a handshake," the store director said. "I really want to tell you how appreciative we are that you stood with us."

—

Tony Aboukhater is an independent contractor who delivers fresh bread to half a dozen Market Basket stores. As he has for eighteen years now, he begins his route each day at around 1 o'clock in the morning; he finishes ten hours later but still well before most people have thought about what they will have for lunch. It's a physically demanding job made all the more difficult by Aboukhater's continuing recovery from knee replacement surgery; the pain makes walking difficult at times.

Aboukhater still remembers the day that Arthur T. Demoulas approached him during one of his deliveries years ago. He was humbled that an executive like Arthur T. would take the time to introduce himself. Years later, he brought his boys Elie and Michael to work. By coincidence, Arthur T. was there and struck up a conversation with them. Arthur T. asked them about their plans for the future and about their schooling. They told him they were studying business in college, one at University of Massachusetts, Lowell and the other at Northern Essex Community College. Arthur T. told them to visit him the next day. When they did, he gave them each a $1 thousand scholarship for their studies. Aboukhater's wife Amal met Arthur T. at a store opening in Haverhill and was impressed with Arthur T.'s humility. She says he still remembers her and her sons by name.

When the protest hit full swing in the summer of 2014, Aboukhater had no doubts about joining those on the picket line. Some of his friends thought he was crazy. They reminded him that he relied on Market Basket for 90 percent of his income—that if the movement were to fail, he would probably be fired as a vendor. But he and Amal believed that without Arthur T. at the helm, "things were not going to be the same at Market Basket."

Amal still gets emotional remembering the protest. She is proud of her participation but also remembers the sacrifices it required. With Market Basket no longer an account, Tony was only delivering to a few restaurants. As an independent contractor, he isn't salaried like many other vendors. Money was tight during that time, and the couple had a mortgage and other bills to pay.

Nevertheless, each day that Tony returned from his short route, Amal would be waiting for him. Most mornings she would have her sneakers on by the time he arrived home, eager to get to the picket line outside the corporate offices in Tewksbury. There were days during which the pain in his knees and back made it difficult to walk. Amal says that on those days, she would offer to go alone but that he would insist on keeping her company. Tony prefers to tease Amal with *his* version of the story, which is that when he'd complain about the pain, she'd say, "Get your ass up; we have to go!" Whose version is more accurate is between Tony and Amal; what is beyond dispute is that the couple picketed nearly every day of the protest in July and August 2014. On days that were particularly painful, Tony would spend much of the day leaning against a large rock holding a sign as Amal walked. The unofficial end of the day happened when Felicia Thornton drove out of the parking lot while being booed by many picketers.

Not every vendor had the same drive to protest, but the feeling of loyalty to friends and colleagues who were involved in the battle for control of the company was fairly commonplace.

—

It seemed that every avenue into or out of Market Basket was now gridlocked. Associates had walked off the job or were demonstrating against the new management. Customers were boycotting, sending sales down by more than 90 percent. Even many vendors joined the fight by cutting off shipments and picketing alongside associates and customers. Yet as the protest dragged on, negotiations to sell the company were at an impasse. Would this struggle require an outside force to resolve it? Some began looking to lawmakers.

14

"Hostages"

On July 19, shortly after the warehouse workers walked off the job and vendors were beginning to halt shipments, Barry Finegold, a state senator representing the Second Essex and Middlesex Districts had an idea. Finegold was running for state treasurer and was attending an event for his campaign. But he couldn't get Market Basket off his mind. He had attended a rally the day before and had been impressed by the passion he saw from associates and customers. He turned to a colleague in the State Senate, Sal DiDomenico. DiDomenico represents the Middlesex and Suffolk Districts, which includes Chelsea, Massachusetts.

"I'm thinking about getting everybody, all the elected officials, to boycott Market Basket."

He showed DiDomenico a write-up inviting lawmakers to pledge support for the movement.

"What do you think?"

"Barry, I think it's a great idea. We should do it."

Within a few days, they had twenty-seven names—names that they read to the thousands of protesters at the following rally. Before long, he had more than 160 names from Massachusetts and New Hampshire. "The thing just took off," Finegold said.

Finegold had grown up in the region. He, like others who signed his petition, had shopped at Market Basket for years. He was hearing from constituents about how important it was to have a Market Basket in the area. "Some people in these communities that live paycheck to paycheck," he explains, "if [they] have another 10 percent increase on their food cost, something gives."

As a lawmaker, Finegold had plenty of experience with partisan politics. Massachusetts is known to be a Democratic territory, but like much of the country, red districts are getting redder and blue districts are getting bluer. Yet on this issue, he found a broad coalition of support. He says, "It was one of the most bipartisan issues that I ever got involved with." For many, he says, it was the story of the courage of associates. Even he says that he might not have gotten involved had it simply been a dispute over benefit pay. Once he saw thousands of workers say, "We are willing to lose our jobs until the CEO gets back into place," he felt he needed to intervene.

Addressing protesters at a rally on July 21, early in the conflict, Finegold put it this way: "The fact that all of you have taken care of our families all these years—well guess what? We're gonna stand with your families now!"

Still, some were critical and said that Finegold and the others who signed his petition were overstepping; this was a private company, and it wasn't the job of the government to choose sides. Finegold ignored these critics because he says, "It was the right thing to do."

Reflecting on this today, Finegold says that "every so often, if the government can help you as a problem solver, I don't think they should shy away from getting involved."

He reached out to Massachusetts Governor Deval Patrick early on, hoping to get him and the full weight of the state government involved. But as we will soon see, it wasn't until the situation reached the brink of disaster that the Massachusetts governor stepped in.

—

Sal DiDomenico, the state senator from Chelsea, attended every rally in Tewksbury and spoke at two of them. As an elected official,

DiDomenico is no stranger to large crowds and public gatherings. But recreating the scene in his mind, DiDomenico was captivated by the protesters' ardor: "To see the sea of people, and they set up tents, they had flags, and they had signs. The money that they spent on their own to buy all that."

He was also impressed by the protesters' unity under difficult circumstances. Every time there was a threat, "they leaned on each other" and seemed to get stronger. "These are people that really need jobs, families, husbands, wives, kids," he said. "They could have lost everything." And in his district, many workers were English-language learners. He says for those workers to "have the courage to stand up" moved him especially.

It also amazed him that customers would be so loyal. He watched as "customers kept coming to the store," not to shop but to stand with the picking workers. The former Everett city councilor saw early on how the Market Basket standoff was different from nearly any other situation a lawmaker would come across; he says, "Everything was unprecedented."

DiDomenico felt so strongly that there were lessons in this movement that he brought his sons, eight and nine years old, to rallies and picket lines. He wanted his boys to see people acting peacefully but forcefully for something they believe in. He hoped to show them "how people can come together to get something done."

While he was at one of the rallies, a member of the senior management team gave one of DiDomenico's sons a stuffed giraffe, the protest symbol that reminds people they need to "stick their necks out." That giraffe stayed by his son's side for months, even after the protests; it is now a fixture next to his son's car seat—a companion on trips, short or long.

—

Another outspoken supporter for the movement was Lowell's state senator Eileen Donoghue. Donoghue knows this community as well as anyone. She previously served on the city council and later was the mayor of Lowell. She remembers that Market Basket was on everyone's mind that summer, not only in Lowell, but also in the smaller surrounding towns to the west that she also represents. Many asked what she could do to help. But still more asked what *they* could do.

When we spoke with Donoghue, several months after the summer showdown, she repeatedly referred to the events of that summer as a "crisis." She worried about what could happen if Market Basket were to go under, but she was also concerned about how people were being affected *during* the protest. "The truth was, there were food shortages," she said. "It was a serious issue."

Some would tell her that it wasn't the place of a politician to get involved in a corporate dispute. She recalls, "People said, 'It's a private matter. It's a private company.' True, it was a private company, but it affects the public good when you're talking about the essentials of life." For example, the Council on Aging in Westford, Massachusetts, serves close to half of all those age sixty or older in that city. Donoghue visited this organization during that time and talked with many of those senior citizens. "It struck me then how critical it was to the seniors who would take a bus from the senior center to a Market Basket," she said. "When that was no longer available, it was a real sacrifice, and it struck a toll for them how big of a sacrifice it was for them."

Despite the challenges, those seniors didn't waver in their support for Market Basket. She was also struck by how much the Market Basket associates loved their jobs. "They were completely committed to the Demoulas family," she said, "and vice versa." As a result, the rallies had a larger significance to New Englanders. She explains, "The message it gave to people was, people matter." "The outcome was never certain," she added, "and the stakes were very high." But Donoghue saw this struggle as being about something larger: "We're going to fight with you because Artie T. has done that for our community and communities across the New England area."

—

While the involvement by state lawmakers in Massachusetts and New Hampshire demonstrated that the movement had broad-based support, the involvement of the governors reflected how critical the situation was. New Hampshire Governor Maggie Hassan, who was re-elected that fall, and Massachusetts Governor Deval Patrick, whose second and final term as governor ended the following January, took an interest in these events largely because the economies of their states would be greatly impacted by the collapse of a multibillion-dollar company.

Hassan moved early on to get involved. The dispute was sending Market Basket toward bankruptcy, and she was concerned that the ripple effect of Market Basket shutting its doors could be devastating on a number of fronts. Her immediate concern was for jobs in the state. Market Basket provides around eight thousand full- and part-time jobs in New Hampshire; it is one of the larger employers in the state.

In an interview in November 2014, Hassan told us, "One of the things you try to do as governor is make sure that you are protecting jobs in your state and helping the private sector create more jobs. It is part of that function." She believed that if the dispute was not settled, the result could be a crisis on the order of magnitude of a major earthquake or a devastating storm. Not only would lost jobs be problematic for those associates out of work, but the numbers of associates in New Hampshire would strain the entire unemployment trust fund, placing it at financial risk. Hassan said, "I liken it to a natural disaster that ripped through my state. If those stores had been flooded or destroyed by weather and all of a sudden all those people had been out of work, we would have tried to support the company in rebuilding. We would have done what we could to help the people who suddenly did not have jobs. To me, it was like a natural disaster caused by family dispute."

She was also concerned for shoppers, especially those for whom Market Basket "makes a difference in their weekly budget." Market Basket has an even greater market share in New Hampshire's largest communities than it does in Massachusetts, so the chain is more embedded in the state's communities. Her office received hundreds of calls over the summer from customers who pressed her administration for what she knew and if she was doing anything to help resolve the standoff. Even more people would approach her at the public events she attended. It was clear that the protest weighed heavily on the minds of her constituents. Even at Hassan's own dinner table, Market Basket came up. Her husband is a "devoted Market Basket shopper" who informed her that the boycott was spreading.

Hassan was committed to being part of the solution, but she couldn't do it alone. Market Basket is a multistate company, and it required a multistate solution. Eyes turned to the government of Massachusetts.

—

Unlike his New Hampshire counterpart, it took longer for Massachusetts's top official, Governor Deval Patrick, to step into the mix. When first asked about his thoughts on the matter, he signaled that he did not wish to take sides. He avoided commenting on the issue as long as he could, but with the protest headlining front pages across his state every day for weeks, there was only so long he could go without stating his opinion. He was finally cornered at a press availability session on August 8, and he deflected with some brief comments: "You know, what we're dealing with here is a dispute over who the boss should be at Market Basket. And that's a serious dispute. It has had a lot of impact on a lot of people, employees and shoppers alike, and I hope that the board sorts that out . . . but the issue with Market Basket . . . is about who the CEO of the company should be, and as I said, that's a private matter and a private family."

The comments angered many of Arthur T.'s supporters. Patrick viewed this as a matter for the board to work out, and since the board was controlled by Arthur S., it came across as tacit support for that side. Then associates discovered that Patrick's wife, Diane, was a managing partner at Ropes & Gray, the prestigious law firm that represented the Market Basket board's three A/B "independent" directors. The coincidental linkage fed suspicion among some.

Over the next few weeks, Governor Patrick tried to stay above the fray. He maintained that this was a private dispute between board members and encouraged the board to work to reach a sale of the company. In Patrick's view, protesters were not alleging unfair labor practices; they simply wanted to choose one CEO over another.

For protesters, this missed the point. Yes, their primary demand was to return Arthur T. as their CEO, but they were really fighting to preserve the culture of Market Basket—a culture that provided good jobs to thousands and affordable groceries to millions. Arthur T. was seen as the embodiment of that culture, and returning him to the executive suite was the surest way to protect it.

In mid-August, after Market Basket's new co-CEOs told store managers to reduce payroll to correspond to the sharp drop in revenue, Patrick made his first detailed public comments about the feud. On August 13, despite Patrick's long reluctance to get involved, he acknowledged that he had spoken with Arthur T., Arthur S., and Keith Cowan, the board of directors' chairman, that day.

Nonetheless, the governor continued to characterize the board as the final decision makers and protesters as acting beyond their jurisdiction, so to speak. In comments days later, the governor enraged associates again by calling on them to return to work. Speaking to reporters at the State House following a press conference, Patrick described associates as being "held hostage to a private dispute." But he also pressed them to end the standoff: "They have it entirely within their power to stabilize the company by going back to work, and I hope they can see a way do that while the buyer and seller work out the final terms of a transaction." His request that associates return to their jobs mirrored statements from shareholders associated with Arthur S. and the independent directors. In fact, the three independent board members released a statement later that afternoon saying they agreed with the governor that workers should return to their jobs.

The associate-managed website "We Are Market Basket" again shot back—this time at the governor. "We will not go back to work when the governor, the board, or any other entity tells us to," the site said. "We will go back to work when Arthur T. Demoulas goes back to work with full authority or when the deal is in place to sell him the company."

Reporters asked the governor his thoughts on likely layoffs of part-time workers, now that sales at Market Basket had all but disappeared. "Well I certainly don't want to see that happen. I can't imagine any citizen wants to see that happen," Patrick said in a press-availability session. "Certainly the workers impacted don't want to see that happen."

For many protesters, the standoff became a political litmus test. And Patrick certainly wasn't the only politician who preferred not to choose sides. Massachusetts Senators Elizabeth Warren and Ed Markey were notably silent on the issue for weeks. Of those two, Warren was criticized especially harshly because she had garnered a reputation for supporting workers' rights. She eventually made a strong statement criticizing the board and the replacement CEOs on August 19 but said she would not involve herself.

—

In the meantime, Arthur T. proposed purchasing the 50.5 percent of Market Basket owned by Arthur S.'s side, and the two sides were in ongoing talks. Arthur T. had made the offer weeks before, and for a few weeks, it was purportedly considered along with the offers made by the Delhaize Group and other national players. But as bidders realized that they would be purchasing a company with disgruntled employees, boycotting customers, and disappearing vendors, some may have dropped out. This appears to have left Arthur T.'s offer as the only viable bid left standing. Moreover, it was at preprotest value and for the full 50.5 percent owned by George's heirs (Arthur S.'s side). Estimates placed the bid around $1.5 billion.

Governor Deval Patrick declined our invitation for an interview. However, we spoke with his chief of staff, Richard Sullivan, about the governor's motivations for joining the process. "The governor was very clear early on that this was not the role of a government to get involved in a private company and a private transaction," Sullivan said. However, he said the effect that the standoff was having, in terms of employment and customers' access to affordable groceries, reached a threshold point for the governor. Market Basket was in dire straits, and an intervention by the governor presented "an opportunity to put it back on its feet." Sullivan said the governor's office "felt there was a role the governor could play—to convene the parties" as someone who wouldn't play favorites. The governor filed a disclosure form earlier that month with the State Ethics Commission in what he called "an abundance of caution" in case the board accepted his offer to help end the stalemate. Patrick stressed in his disclosure that Ropes & Gray represented board members, not the company.

Hassan says, "We offered to meet with them, but we could not insist." There was deep mistrust between the two sides, and eventually both sides agreed to meet with the two governors in the hope that an independent voice with additional clout could help bridge the gap. Sullivan adds that once asked "to play that role, [Patrick] was happy to do it."

"[The governors] put their capital on the line," said Scott Latham, a University of Massachusetts, Lowell, business professor who was following the case closely.

On August 17, Arthur S., Arthur T., Governor Hassan, and their respective representatives were hosted at Governor Patrick's satellite office in the western Massachusetts city of Springfield. Unfortunately, this gathering ended with little progress, and the respective teams went back to their daily negotiations. The next two weeks involved grueling closed-door bargaining, which became quite heated.

On August 22, Governors Hassan and Patrick released a joint statement reporting, "All parties report that they are optimistic that an agreement will be reached." The Governors said, "We are hopeful that employees will return to work, and the stores will reopen, early next week." The proclamation offered a glimmer of hope to a weary collection of associates, customers, and vendors. But the deal wasn't complete yet.

15

"I Am in Awe of What You Have All Accomplished"

As August neared an end, the ever-expanding movement was still fighting but exhausted. For six long weeks, picketers had endured nineteen days of summer heat. They had gathered by the thousands at multiple rallies in Tewksbury and at smaller impromptu gatherings around Massachusetts, New Hampshire, and Maine. Close to two million customers were still scrambling for food; many simply went to competitor supermarkets, but others pieced together their menus from various farmstands and local merchants. Vendors watched and waited, some facing major disruptions to their cash flow.

A breakthrough seemed close at hand. Governors Hassan and Patrick released a statement saying they were optimistic and that they expected to "restore Arthur T. to operating authority on an interim basis until the sale closes."

But there remained obstacles, not the least of which was the lack of trust between the two cousins. Experts in family business knew why nothing was happening quickly: the negotiations, and the broader saga itself, were about far more than business. "These decisions are never just business-driven—never," said Jeffrey Davis, chairman of the consulting group Mage LLC and cofounder of the

Family Business Association. "There's too much history, emotion, and jealousy."

Associates were hopeful but guardedly so. Tom Trainor, the district supervisor and a leader of the movement to bring back Arthur T., says he was concerned that Arthur S.'s side would "pull a Lucy"; it was a reference to the classic Peanuts cartoon in which Charlie Brown goes to kick the football, and Lucy promises to hold it for him but then pulls the ball away at the last moment, leaving Charlie Brown to fall on his back after kicking nothing. Trainor and others were worried that Arthur S.'s side would return Arthur T. to his executive position only long enough to stabilize the company and sell it to Delhaize or another bidder.

Doubts began to surface, and experts struggled to interpret the signals that trickled out of the negotiations. "When people say, 'I'm more than willing to sell but have to agree to other terms,' that signals to me they don't really want to sell," observed Ed Tarlow, a cofounder of the Family Business Association. The region held its breath, and protesters watched helplessly as rumors ricocheted across social media. Board meetings were scheduled, then cancelled, then rescheduled again.

In the fifth week, some senior managers were saying, "We're on the goal line," meaning that a deal was within reach—figuratively just a few yards away. The expression caught on. But then days went by with no forward progress. After about a week, concerned warehouse workers asked Dean Joyce, the warehouse manager of the first shift, what was going on.

"I thought they said we were on the goal line?"

In typical fashion, Joyce lightened the mood with humor.

"Look, some of these people aren't as big sports fans as us," he said. "When they said we were on the goal line, they didn't realize what side of the field we were on. They thought we had five yards to go; we really had ninety-five yards to go. Guys, stay strong!"

Vendor Jim Fantini says he was cognizant that "the world was watching [them] in an almost voyeuristic sense: 'What these guys are doing is crazy. They are walking a tightrope. Are they going to make it across?'"

For many, it was almost too much to endure. Diane Patterson worked in the main offices as a supervisor of refrigeration. She is normally even-keeled, but the roller-coaster ride of the negotiations made the days of the fifth and sixth weeks of the protest especially difficult. "Every day, you had no idea what tomorrow would bring. You would hear that we're close, and then nothing," she remembers. Patterson was thankful for the support she got in the community, but that support was also a constant reminder of the ongoing dispute. "People would say [excitedly], 'oh, you work for Market Basket!' But I'm freaking out." Patterson and her colleagues "were clinging to social media for news of anything." They would also observe anything out of the ordinary in case it was a sign of a breakthrough: "If we saw extra news trucks, we'd say, ah, maybe today we're going to hear something."

The evening of August 26 brought disturbing news. The board reportedly made a contingency plan to close sixty-one stores to stem the bleeding. If the chain shuttered these stores, there was no guarantee they would ever reopen. Was this simply posturing—an empty threat? Or was it the final sign that the talks were stalled, possibly for good?

Senior managers say that the announcement loomed overhead for the next twenty-four hours, making them some of the most difficult of the entire protest. Not only was the closure of sixty-one stores worrisome, but an afternoon board meeting to discuss the details of a deal had dismantled in minutes. Joe Schmidt says it "made [him] question what the true intention of the board [was]." Tom Trainor described himself as "fit to be tied." It seemed that all they had worked for was about to crumble—that the board and the new CEOs were about to dig in for a fight that could last many months. It could spell the end of the company that so many loved.

—

Then, suddenly, on the evening of August 27, a deal materialized from what seemed like thin air. Word began leaking that an agreement on a sale appeared to be reached. There had been false alarms before, but news outlets were all confirming an accord. This was for real.

At 11:19 P.M., through a spokeswoman, Arthur T. made the announcement so many were waiting for. The company was—subject to financing—once again his.

The official statement read, "Market Basket and its shareholders are pleased to announce today that the Market Basket shareholders have entered into a binding agreement pursuant to which the Class B shareholders will acquire the 50.5% ownership interest of Market Basket currently owned by the Class A shareholders." Arthur T. and his management team would be returning to their day-to-day operational authority. The new CEOs, Thornton and Gooch, would remain in a monitoring role until the deal closed several months later but with little to no decision-making authority. It would be a form of suspended animation.

Not surprisingly, as news stations broke the news all over New England, associates, vendors, customers, and other supporters shot text messages and phone calls back and forth. Many workers said they were so eager to return to work that they barely bothered to get sleep that night. Joe Garon, a grocery buyer who was fired at the start of the protest, got a call at 2 A.M. and was at work within four hours. "I slept an hour here and there," he said.

—

Dean Joyce, a warehouse manager, was worried that if he arrived too early, he might be arrested for trespassing on Market Basket property; he had been fired by the replacement CEOs six weeks before. After conferring with other senior managers, he decided to wait until midnight before entering the building.

Warehouse worker Luis Mendez heard the news at around 10 P.M. He got a call from a friend who said it was over. Mendez wasn't sure whether to believe it or not. He turned on the evening news to make sure. Less than thirty minutes after a local station confirmed it, he was in his car driving from his home in Lawrence to the warehouse in Tewksbury.

Kenneth Sweeney, a truck driver and thirty-year employee, said he got the call to return to work at 3:15 A.M. He was up and at the warehouse within a half hour. Jovannie Ferrer and Alex Cruz, two other warehouse workers, were at headquarters before 8 A.M. Their shifts didn't start until 3 P.M. "I can't wait to get in there and punch in," Ferrer said at the time. Cruz added, "We're like kids on Christmas."

The warehouse was in disarray. But the crew began working within an hour. By the next day, pundits were already raining on the parade, claiming that it would take months to return Market Basket operations to their former state. Joyce and his warehouse workers took it as a challenge.

They found the last order that had been placed several weeks prior—it had not yet been filled. They began the selection process immediately. Meanwhile, Joyce set out to find and bring back every truck the company had. Some were still blocking loading docks at stores. He needed to gather and account for every resource he had.

Joyce used every asset available. To fill the order, each person found a role and worked through the night. By sunrise, smiles were still wide, and they had made progress. They continued working around the clock for days. "The work we did in those [first] four days, it was awesome." According to Joyce, stores were fully stocked with groceries within a week. The following week, they conducted a full inventory.

—

The scene was just as happy in the offices fifty yards away. Barbara Paquette, the accounts payable supervisor, got a text message at around 1 A.M. telling her that workers could arrive whenever they wanted. She entered the building at around 3:30 that morning. The building was decorated, she says. Steve Paulenka, whose primary job at Market Basket is to open new stores, treated this as a grand reopening of the Market Basket corporate offices. He and others had taken dozens of protest signs from across the street and used them to decorate the insides of the offices.

It was a festive sight: "We were all crying and hugging each other and high-fiving," Paquette said. "It was just great."

Like others, Paquette said she went straight to work after hearing the news. But she said she found that the files were a mess. "Accounts payable was all over the building. It was in a conference room, in the CEOs room, they found it in a box out back. It was a disaster." Accounts receivable was in similarly bad shape. The new CEOs and their undersized crew had been overwhelmed by the paperwork involved with keeping the company afloat.

It took several weeks to square the books again, but moods in the offices remained positive. There was a constant stream of greeting cards, flowers, and fruit baskets from well-wishers across New England.

—

In most stores, the celebration did not start until the next morning when customers began to arrive by the hundreds. Associates greeted customers at the door to thank them. Customers hugged associates. Some customers didn't care what they bought as long as it helped get Market Basket on its feet again. One post to the "Save Market Basket" Facebook page read, "See you at 7 A.M. tomorrow to buy anything on the shelves!!!! I don't even have a dog but I'll buy dog food if needed!!"

Al Gerrato, a ninety-three-year-old customer in Portsmouth, New Hampshire, said, "It becomes part of your family." He described the conflict as a "war." It felt like "the end of the war." He said, "Shopping anywhere else would mean letting down your family, you feel like you just can't stop at any other place, you have to come to Market Basket."

There was literally dancing in the aisles at one store. A couple hundred shoppers organized—with the help of the store director in Londonderry, New Hampshire—what one might describe as part flash mob, part conga line. Customers cheered and danced triumphantly while the Pharrell Williams song "Happy" blared from the public address system.

A few days later, warehouse worker David Courteau was shopping at that same Market Basket in Londonderry. The person at the deli counter greeted him warmly and welcomed him back, thanking him for boycotting along with other customers. Courteau said that it was especially nice to be back because he worked in the warehouse. She said, "Come here, I want to give you a hug!" Then she called Store Director Mark Lemieux, who gathered other employees to thank Courteau and his wife for all they sacrificed.

—

On Friday, Arthur T.'s return made the front page on at least a dozen newspapers in Massachusetts, six in New Hampshire, and two more in Maine. Market Basket had become the story across greater Boston and a big swath of New England over the summer.

The *New York Times*—which called it "one of the strangest labor actions in American business history"—wrote about the boycott on at least four occasions. Slate, CNN Money, and *Esquire* published their own stories about the saga, the *Wall Street Journal* had several op-eds, and the *Washington Post* wrote about the boycott on its "On Leadership" blog. NBC *Nightly News* ran a segment about Market Basket in late July, and fired Market Basket District Supervisor Tom Trainor appeared on *All In with Chris Hayes* on MSNBC a few days after the *Nightly News* segment.

In the autumn following the sale agreement, at least two documentaries were in the works (*Market Basket Saga* and *Food Fight*).

—

On the morning of Arthur T.'s return, there was yet another large gathering on East Street, the home of Market Basket's headquarters. But this one was moved across the street from where earlier ones had taken place. Now it was on company property. Arthur T. was about to address his associates, and a few people started to ready a lectern on the stairs of the head office.

"No, no, no," said Steve Paulenka, who had waited more than a year for this moment. "We're gonna put my truck in the back." It was the same truck that was used in the rallies in Tewksbury; the same truck from which dozens of associates, politicians, customers, and vendors had spoken; and the same truck that had traveled thousands of miles for many weeks, visiting stores around the region. Paulenka told Demoulas in 2013 that one day he was going to give his victory speech from the back of that truck, and he wasn't going to miss this chance.

Arthur T. Demoulas made a triumphant return, arriving early to find a crowd already gathered and waiting for him. Chants that were once "Who do we want? ATD! And when do we want him? Now!" were now "Who do we have? ATD!"

It was the first time they had seen him in many weeks. He was tired, but relieved, and somewhat uncomfortable with being the center of attention. Characteristically, he deflected the praise.

"As I stand before you, I am in awe of what you have all accomplished," he began, "and the sterling example you have all set for so many people across the region and across the country." The big stuffed giraffe was right at his side. Some managers were back in suits and ties, whereas others still had their t-shirts with slogans like "Market Basket strong."

"The public watched in awe and admiration because you empowered others to seek change," he said. Seeing everyone again, he said, was like "a little piece of heaven on earth." Some associates interrupted with shouts of "We love you."

"I love you too."

He continued, "May we always remember this past summer first as a time where our collective values of loyalty, courage and kindness toward one another really prevailed, and in that process we just happened to save our company . . . You have demonstrated to the world that it is a person's moral obligation and social responsibility to protect a culture that provides an honorable and a dignified place in which to work."

PART FOUR

Reflecting on this movement, Jay Childs still can't get over "the sheer audacity of it." Childs is a New England Emmy-winning filmmaker and the owner of the production company JBC Communications. He was taken with the Market Basket story enough to devote two years to making a documentary about it. From the moment he saw Arthur T. arrive at a rally in 2013—shortly after the board of directors had just shifted in favor of Arthur S.—he knew that he was witnessing something special. Associates gathered around him "like he was a rock star or the pope or something. . . . They revered him." Childs was struck by the connection that associates felt with this man. He felt he was witnessing "something historic" and wanted to understand what made so many people so loyal to him and the company.

Though he was drawn immediately to the movement, senior managers were not instantly welcoming of him. At first, they looked at Childs with a degree of suspicion. But over the course of months, Childs was able to demonstrate to Market Basket loyalists that he wasn't looking for a scoop for that evening's news—that he wanted to tell the unvarnished story. Eventually, he gained untethered access to the movement. He was "embedded" with the Market Basket troops, attending nearly every rally, picket line, and job fair. He later teamed up with colleague and fellow producer Melissa Paly, forming a two-person crew that continued to follow the story, even after the initial deal had been signed, and traveling to Washington, D.C., as senior managers met with the secretary of labor, for example.

Childs was so tenacious in following the story because he believed it struck a nerve with so many people. He says that "time and time again," corporate mergers and buyouts are made in the interest of shareholders alone, sometimes affecting people's lives in profound ways. Wages may be cut and jobs may be lost. Although conditions may be marginally worse, individuals feel powerless to do much about it. They "lift their head up for a while," but with seemingly little choice, they "put their head back down" and return to work. Market Basket is a case, he says, in which associates, customers, and others came together and took a strong stand in unison, "winning out over what was a fixed narrative."

It is an inspiring story that we can all learn from. Hundreds of Market Basket loyalists agree; they chipped in more than $65 thousand on crowdfunding site Kickstarter to help fund the film. It was scheduled for release in the second half of 2015.

—

There was one Boston-area businessperson who closely followed the Market Basket story. Eliot Tatelman was interested because, for years, he ran another iconic New England business that was started by his grandfather in 1917: Jordan's Furniture. Those in the region would instantly recognize the voices of Eliot and his brother Barry from radio advertisements that ran for decades.

We spoke to Tatelman about the challenges of running a family business like Market Basket. "In some respects," Tatelman says, "it's more difficult running a business with a family member than anyone else." For example, he and his brother had different personalities: "He's much more outgoing. He'd like to be at the head of the table giving a speech. I'd like to be in the back of the room just listening." In fact, Barry left the company in 2006 to pursue a career as a Broadway producer, leaving Eliot to run the company on his own (although since 1999, it is a subsidiary of Berkshire Hathaway). But in the end, they made it work during their years together because they understood each other, and he adds, "In the big picture, it makes it more rewarding."

"Life is more important than business and fighting over the almighty dollar," Tatelman says. And that is why he watched the rallies for Arthur T. in awe. "Of course," he says, "Everyone in my position, when they saw that, they said, 'what if that was me, what would they do?' I hope to never find out."

His impressions went beyond Market Basket to broad business ideals in general, he said. "It goes deeper than just Market Basket. It makes you think, number one, about life in general and what you want from it. And, number two, if you're running a business, what do you want out of it? What does it mean to you?" He says, "The secret's not how to do it, but what's within you."

He says that Arthur T. likely realized long ago that it's a people business. The company could make more money in the short term if profit margins were the only priority, but it wouldn't have lasted long. "In the meantime, he's building something so incredible, it can just keep growing," he said. "My hat's off to the guy."

—

For Market Basket, almost one hundred years of continual supply of groceries to the New England region was punctuated by a year-long protest and six weeks of complete shutdown. The protest is over, but the company continues. Now the company transitions back to its usual operations, even opening four new stores in the months following the protest. Speaking at an event a month after the protest ended, Arthur T. renewed his commitment to the Market Basket business model: "We go forward with a commitment to go forward and grow a socially responsible company that, at all times, is focused on the well-being and best interests of the associates, the customers, the vendors, and the communities that we serve."

What he describes is not so much a destination but a continual effort to maintain a business that improves lives.

Market Basket is being watched not just for whether it will continue to thrive but also because it continues to offer lessons.

Progress at Market Basket will not be easy. Challenges remain. This is a difficult industry in the best of circumstances. Market Basket has some tremendous assets from which it can draw, but it also will have to overcome a few headwinds.

16

Challenges Ahead

Market Basket is still a privately held company, so exact figures are not available on the final deal to sell 50.5 percent of the company. Estimates put the transaction in the vicinity of $1.5 billion. It also appears that around two-thirds of that total is borrowed from a number of investment banks. That would mean that the company now has debt totaling more than $1 billion. To put this in perspective, a home mortgage of $1 billion at a 4 percent interest rate would require a monthly payment of about $4.7 million (more than $150 thousand per day).

"We've never been exposed to debt," says Bill Marsden. "It's something we have to learn to handle." For a company with seventy-five stores, each of which makes a million or more dollars per week, handling the day-to-day finances of that debt is probably manageable.

What makes the debt more challenging in this circumstance is that the commitment to pay down that debt could affect other relationships that Arthur T. and his management team value. Arthur T. undoubtedly feels that he owes many associates, vendors, and customers for their support throughout the protest. Some of those people may have expectations that Arthur T. will be as generous as they have grown to expect. The additional debt places some financial pressure on that wealth sharing.

Take, for example, the 4 percent discount for customers that was in effect for a full year. After all the customer's coupons were accounted for, an additional 4 percent was taken off his or her total at the register. The discount was instituted in January 2014. Not surprisingly, it was very popular with consumers. But it was scheduled to end at the end of 2014, and Market Basket let it fade away as scheduled and without fanfare. Customers were disappointed but ultimately were accommodating in letting it go. They understood the fiscal pressure that Market Basket was facing, even as they continued to bargain hunt.

There are also great expectations from associates. Many of those associates went to bat for Arthur T. and his management philosophy. They fought for the combination of respect in the workplace and wealth sharing. That respect remains unchanged, and profit sharing and bonuses continue. Despite all the lost sales over six weeks during the summer, the company managed to pay out $46 million in year-end bonuses—more than it did in 2013. The bonuses were perhaps as much a thank-you as they were an indication of how much Market Basket brought in for the year. Arthur T. wrote to employees while giving out the bonuses, calling 2014 "a defining year for our company."

Associates are thankful, but there is a sort of anticipation that those bonuses will keep coming at the same pace they have in the past. In the months and years ahead, the debt will constrain Arthur T. and his management team somewhat.

It is important not to overstate this challenge. The loyalty that associates, vendors, and customers have to Market Basket goes beyond money. Much of the loyalty stems from the respect that many feel they get when dealing with Market Basket. Fair wages and low prices are just signals that the company values each person. In the worst-case scenario, if Market Basket is not able to sustain bonuses and other discounts, there are still other ways to communicate and deliver the same respect, as they have done over the years. However, as Boston University Professor James Post says, "The money is going to be tighter," adding another challenge to the Market Basket team.

—

Part of Market Basket's success stems from its policy of promoting from within. Managers gain intimate knowledge of Market Basket's systems and ways of doing things. Associates have respect for their supervisors because they know that they once did their job.

But there is swelling pressure from the bottom for promotions. Most stores have a number of associates who already excel in their jobs and are waiting for an opening somewhere else in the company. Because the turnover of associates is so low, jobs open up infrequently. The best shot at a promotion comes when a new store opens. But even a new store opening may only offer fifteen to twenty positions, such as store director, assistant store director, or department head. Moreover, as the company's footprint grows, the available jobs through these store openings will require associates to relocate farther and farther away. Many associates hungry for a promotion are willing to move in order to prove their desire to advance, but it is still a lot to ask, especially if the associate has a family.

Meanwhile, competition is becoming more and more intense. Wegmans has entered New England with a model that has been extremely successful in other regions. Walmart, Target, and other retailers continue to push into the grocery business, creating additional pressure.

Managers realize this and feel a certain pressure to continue expanding so that everyone has a development path. Bill Marsden puts it better than anyone: "Can you imagine being an assistant manager for ten years? You have the ability to manage a store, but we don't have an opening for them because nobody wants to leave. It forces us to grow. We gotta get off our ass and build stores. We have a responsibility to [those associates]."

The blessing of loyalty creates an urgency to grow. Customers buy more, stores do well, associates are rewarded and promoted, another store opens, and customers buy more. It is a winning formula as long as customers keep coming. Of course, when success depends on a cycle like this, it also creates vulnerability. If things break down at any point, everyone is affected.

Competition is more likely to intensify than to ease over the coming years. Senior managers seem to have an intuitive sense that the key to addressing this challenge is to keep that virtuous cycle strong by fostering strong relationships among associates and customers. Market Basket has a seasoned management team and a strong culture that should keep them steady for the foreseeable future.

—

The protest changed relationships between associates at Market Basket, mostly for the better. On the positive side, it brought together associates who were unlikely to interact otherwise. Associates say that the experience showed them another side of colleagues to whom they were not previously close. "Standing out there for six weeks, you saw their true colors," said warehouse worker David Corteau. Dean Joyce says that before the protest, some office workers held a stereotype of what he jokingly calls "the animals in the warehouse." Joyce even took some offense to it. "Now all the girls in the office are out talking with the guys [from the warehouse] every day. They wave to each other. It gave a personality to the face. They're buddies now. It's amazing."

But some tensions also emerged. A handful of office and warehouse workers crossed the picket line during the protest. None of these associates were fired when Market Basket reopened; most still remain employed by the company today. To say the least, their presence makes for an awkward environment.

Tensions were especially high in the first few weeks after the deal was reached. There were shouting matches and some skirmishes in the warehouse. Joyce and other supervisors had to intervene. They called meetings during which they stressed the importance of staying disciplined and focused on the ultimate goal of serving customers. It worked to stop the fighting, but an animosity still smolders between those who walked out and those who stayed. Says one associate in the warehouse, "We look at it like if you were to come out here with us, we probably could have been back here earlier [ending the walkout].

Would it have? I don't know. But that's how it [is viewed]. And it's going to stay that way forever." Another warehouse worker says that he hasn't spoken with an associate in the warehouse who used to be a close friend. Looking back on that former friend who crossed the line, he says, "Maybe we didn't have as much in common as we thought." Nevertheless, it is clear that the lost friendship still hurts.

In offices and stores, the tension is less dramatic but just as real. One associate feels that to place a bumper sticker on a car that says "Arthur T. is our CEO!" is hypocritical for those associates who did little to support the movement during the summer. That associate says that coworkers don't respect them: "There were people who weren't on board [during the protest]. And it made it very difficult. You can't fight with them. You just have to not let it get to you. It's their right. It's hard to look at some people now . . . you know that this one never stood down on the corner with a sign. She never did the work or anything, but yet she still reaps all the benefits of this great company . . . they'll always be kind of an outcast."

Most associates who struggle with this tension tell us they remain professional and just do not engage those people more than they have to. They try to be understanding of the fact that each person has his or her own reasons for his or her choices. One supervisor says that many of those who crossed now regret their decision: "You got a couple of them now; they say, 'I was afraid. If I could have done it all over again, I would have went.' But you know, it's too late now." But those who crossed the line sometimes took some actions that were hurtful to picketers. For example, some helped organize job fairs designed to replace picketers. Those wounds run deep.

Some who crossed the line now claim that others have made work difficult for them since the protest. The tensions run both ways. One associate who did picket sums it up this way: "They want us to apologize for making it difficult for them, and we want them to apologize to us."

The protest created lasting bonds that are helping Market Basket grow. But it also created a fault line that can make work uncomfortable at times. The wounds will heal over time, and the tension is minor compared to the goodwill that the protest seems to have generated.

—

Market Basket has an unconventional streak. However, it is also a traditional company in many ways—in the complexion of its management, for instance. The current board and executive team are mostly male. That sort of imbalance can be found at almost all major companies in the United States and abroad. In fact, consulting giant McKinsey recently found that women account for only 16 percent of the members of executive teams in the United States, 12 percent of those in the United Kingdom, and 6 percent of those in Brazil. Still, Market Basket has ground to gain. All five members of the new board created after Arthur T.'s side of the family took full ownership were men.

To their credit, senior managers realize this and are open to change. Executives hope that in the future, all associates look more like the customers they serve. We've found no evidence of any hostilities toward women or minorities. Rather, senior managers will often intersperse interviews with asides about how the company's meritocracy is rewarding many exceptional women and minorities who are moving up the ranks.

"We've come a million miles in terms of women and minorities," says Cindy Whelan, one of two female store directors in the chain. When asked about how things are changing at Market Basket, she quickly turns to her own experience. She says her husband also worked at Market Basket as a manager until they had their third child. At that point, they realized that they were each working more than sixty hours a week, and "someone else [was] raising [their] children." He decided to leave his job to take care of the kids, while she continues as a store director. She believes that because others in the company have multiple family members working at Market Basket, they are faced with similar choices.

The policy of promoting from within has many advantages for Market Basket, yet it again creates a challenge. It is difficult to quickly change the makeup of the workforce. At the time of writing, there are six women at the store-director or assistant-manager level across Market Basket's seventy-five stores. However, there are forty-one women on the cusp of management, in positions such as head clerk. They make up a growing pool of female associates from which the next generation of assistant managers will be chosen. It will probably be some time before many female and minority department heads are promoted to assistant store manager, then to store director, and finally to jobs that fill the shoes of Tom Trainor or other senior managers.

—

At its core, the movement to "save Market Basket" was defined by the desire to protect a culture, a culture that valued resourcefulness among the Market Basket family to serve the community through the grocery business. Associates, customers, vendors, and others were fighting because they believed that selling the company to an outside bidder would starve that culture. In short, those many stakeholders did not want the company changed.

The resolve of all those stakeholders is admirable, but there is, of course, another side to the coin. Companies must change to survive. They must sometimes reinvent themselves in order to keep up with a dynamic market place.

How will associates and customers react if management needs to shift direction? For example, part of the new model at Market Basket is to have cafés where people can gather before shopping or simply for an afternoon break. Market Basket wants to be more of a destination, a possible alternative to, say, Dunkin Donuts. In this sense, it is adapting a tactic of Wegmans and other chains that seek to keep customers in the stores for more extended periods of time. The move to introduce cafés has been smooth, but in the future, the chain may have to reexamine the way it does business in unforeseen ways. If those changes are more drastic, it may be challenging to convince associates and customers to come along for the ride.

To be clear, protesters were fighting to protect the Market Basket culture, not a café or the sale of a new product line. The point is that if

Market Basket ever needs to pivot dramatically in the future—perhaps even one day after Arthur T.'s tenure as CEO—there may be a contingent of people who are so committed to this current model that those efforts could be slowed down. Fortunately, the fact that resourcefulness is a pillar of the culture bodes well for the company when that change will become necessary.

17

Lessons

If there is one thing that most business people seem to agree on these days, it's that a company is owned by its shareholders. And so the wisdom goes, it is the responsibility of everyone affiliated with the company to make sure that it is run in the best interest of those shareholders and owners. This line of thinking is often presented as a simple fact—an article of faith.

The Market Basket story may give pause to rethink this idea.

Actually, Market Basket is but one piece of evidence in an ongoing debate that has been going on for decades. Way back in the 1930s, two heavyweight scholars—one from Harvard and the other from Columbia—squared off in the pages of the *Harvard Law Review*. It was an intellectual wrestling match between two Ivy League rivals. Adolph Berle, a professor at Columbia University, argued for shareholders. He wrote that "all powers granted to a corporation . . . [are] at all times exercisable only for the ratable benefit of the shareholders." Merrick Dodd, his opponent and a professor at Harvard University responded that "the business corporation . . . is an economic institution which has a social service as well as a profit making function."

Each view has held sway at various times since then. For a time, it seemed that Dodd's multistakeholder concept was winning the battle of ideas. Even Berle graciously conceded sometime later that the issue was settled "squarely in favor of Professor Dodd's contention."

But then, in the 1970s, some economists and finance scholars became concerned that if executives could pursue goals other than profits, there was no telling where it might lead. Those executives might use the company's money to enrich themselves or spend it on things that the shareholders don't care about. This led to the idea that a board of directors needs to be set up so that it watches over the CEO. According to Eugene Fama, a professor at the University of Chicago and a leading voice in the so-called Chicago School, boards need to keep the CEO in check and reward the CEO in ways that encourage acting on the behalf of shareholders. That's why so many public companies reward executives with stock options these days. The idea is to give them an incentive to increase the stock price; it also provides a simple measure of how well they are performing.

Today the pendulum is swinging back to the idea that shareholders are only one of many groups that should benefit from a company. Recent thought is that overemphasizing driving up stock value for shareholders can lead companies down a dangerous path of chasing short-term profits over long-term performance.

The idea that companies need to serve a range of people has even won over some who were once proponents of the shareholder idea. Jack Welch is one of these. He was one of the most successful CEOs of General Electric in the 1980s and 1990s. He was once held up as a hero who was willing to do whatever it took to generate value for shareholders. But now he says, "On the face of it, shareholder value is the dumbest idea in the world. Shareholder value is a result, not a strategy . . . Your main constituencies are your employees, your customers and your products."

Miguel Padro of the Aspen Institute, a nonpartisan organization that helps many of the world's largest companies think about their role in society, says that "business schools have been prolific at imparting" the idea of shareholders as the only true owners of a company. He says that the idea works well for some companies but that "we've kind of reached into the limits of [those] assumptions." He says that the story of Market Basket "really tests the assumptions and shows that there might be something more to the story." It may be time to expand our thinking and bring a wider cross-section of people to the decision-making table.

Cornell Law School Professor Lynn Stout is a leading scholar who is questioning the very idea that shareholders own the company. She explains that the US Supreme Court has recently ruled that a corporation is an entity unto itself, similar to a person. This gives corporations a certain independence and the same free speech that a person enjoys. She says that cases like *Citizens United v. FEC* and *Burwell v. Hobby Lobby* hold up this idea. In the *Citizens United* case, the court ruled that corporations are covered by the First Amendment and can express political views. In the *Burwell* case, the court extended freedom of religion rights to a closely held arts and crafts company on the grounds that it is its own entity. Stout explains that a person cannot own a company any more than a person can own another person. "Because of the legal 'personhood' of corporations," she says, "buying a share in a corporation is like making a contract with the legal 'person' that is the company, which is different from buying the company."

What this means is that we can't look at companies as simply giant sole-proprietorships in which shareholders have total control. A corporation like Market Basket is a different sort of animal.

But if shareholders don't own the company, then who does? If you ask Market Basket's associates, customers, and vendors, they might tell you that *they* do. They love Market Basket and everything they believe it stands for. They give it their hard work, their loyalty, and their purchases. This gives them the right to call some of the shots.

"My life has been spent building this company," says Mark Owens, a longtime employee and manager of the Stratham, New Hampshire, store. "We own it." Calls like his resonated throughout the protest: "This is our company!" "We will only work for Arthur T. Demoulas." Obviously, they recognize that they can't take over the day-to-day operations of the company. But they do believe that they can act as a safeguard when the company's culture comes under attack.

In a sense, the protesters were operating on a sort of psychological ownership. They felt that they could help steer the company because they care about it more than anyone else. The fact that they succeeded could represent a turning point in how we think about corporate ownership. Employees, customers, and suppliers at other companies have a voice. Even if they do not own stock in the company, they can still have a say in how the company is run.

—

Just as important, we need to rethink the role of boards. Jim Fantini, the vendor who took such an active role in the Market Basket protest, points out that the so-called independent members of the board took a potentially dangerous view of their duties. He says that those directors, Keith Cowan, Ron Weiner, and Eric Gebaide, represented only some of the shareholders (Arthur S.'s side) and seemed to never consider the impact their decisions would have on the company or the region. "In my opinion, what these guys were willing to do to inflict on the communities here is on the verge of being criminal." Those board members appeared to act only in the interests of majority shareholders, "essentially ignoring a year's worth of appeals from thousands of stakeholders who would be adversely affected by their actions," Fantini says.

The way Massachusetts Institute of Technology management professor Thomas Kochan sees it, "the Board performed very poorly" because some directors took such a narrow view of their roles as serving shareholders that they almost allowed an otherwise healthy business to fail. "The so-called independent members were not doing their job," he says, "or they wouldn't have let the value of the company continue to decline for every day that the walkout continued."

Common wisdom is that because boards are elected by shareholders, they are charged only with protecting shareholders. That view is misguided and potentially harmful. It is also wrong.

At almost all corporations—Market Basket included—board members have a fiduciary responsibility to serve the *corporation*. Make no mistake: shareholders are part of the extended enterprise and, in fact, have a special place and importance in a corporation. However, shareholders are one of many stakeholders a board needs to consider in its decisions. This responsibility is stated clearly in the Massachusetts Corporate Code, which sets guidelines for companies that are incorporated in the state (as is Market Basket). The code states that each director is expected to serve in good faith, use appropriate and reasonable judgment, and act "in a manner the director reasonably believes to be *in the best interests of the corporation*" (emphasis added). In determining what is in the best interest of the corporation, "A director may consider the interests of the corporation's employees, suppliers, creditors and customers, the economy of the state, the region and the nation, community and societal considerations, and the long-term and short-term interests of the corporation and its shareholders, including the possibility that these interests may be best served by the continued independence of the corporation."

Notice that in this list, the shareholders are given no special preference or status. They are simply among the many people who ought to be considered. The board's duty is larger than simply acting on behalf of those shareholders. The board is there to protect the corporation. In fact, there may be times—and many at Market Basket argue persuasively that this was one of them—when the board must protect the corporation from some of the very shareholders who elected them.

It is perhaps time to expect more from our boards. The board is the custodian of the corporation—or at least it should be thought of that way. In the case of Market Basket, we cannot know the intentions of the independent board members. However, it is difficult to argue that their actions rose to this expectation. It is difficult to argue that something is in the interest of the corporation when it is so vehemently opposed by the vast majority of associates, more than 90 percent of customers, a large swath of vendors, and dozens of lawmakers. The value of Market

Basket is largely embedded in its unique culture, so part of the board's responsibility is to protect that culture.

—

The CEO of Whole Foods, John Mackey, is fond of saying that "business is under attack." The cofounder of the 350-store chain claims that wide swaths of the country believe that business is harmful to society. He cites polls that show a dismal approval rating for big business. Given the backdrop of protests against the 1 percenters—those with a net worth among the top 1 percent in the country—it's easy to think that most people are against profitable businesses in general. This should be especially strong in Massachusetts, a state that has, according to one study, one of the top ten highest income disparities in the country. (New Hampshire ranked twenty-eighth on the list.)

But consider the case of Market Basket. Was the protest movement opposed to the company? On the contrary, protesters believed they were fighting *for* the company. They wanted to restore it, not bring it down. And what about Arthur T. Demoulas? He is a billionaire and among the top 1 percent in the country. In fact, he is much wealthier than the vast majority of those in the 1 percent. However, the protest movement did not denigrate his wealth; rather, it celebrated his success as a manager.

No, this movement was powered by the concern that the company they loved would be taken away from them. The associates, vendors, and customers who coalesced into a movement were undeniably probusiness. Not only do they tolerate the success of Market Basket, they want to contribute to it. Many view the company's growth as a sign that what they believe in is worthwhile and is catching on. The more it grows, the more the company has a chance to impact people's lives.

Early on in the protest of 2014, some pundits claimed that the protest would tarnish the reputation of the company. What those pundits did not consider was that, even at the height of the protest, Market Basket's reputation was sterling. Associates, customers, and vendors always thought highly of the company. The only reputations that became tarnished during the protest were those of some board members and the new CEOs.

It is not business that is under attack; it is greed and dishonesty that people abhor. And what people often encounter in the business world is "short-term, self-interested owners and corporate executives," Kochan said. That sort of behavior has led to a marketplace in which shoppers feel that they are squeezed for every penny and that their value to the company is only measured in dollar terms.

The Market Basket case shows that some people will fight for a business that they believe serves an important purpose—one that promotes fairness and respect. People like to see socially responsible companies succeed as long as they see that the company's actions as genuine and not some sort of window dressing.

—

Market Basket challenges the traditional wisdom of what the boundaries of a company are. Most textbooks portray companies as simple structures with clear boundaries. The insiders are the employees, managers, and investors (who, it is argued, own the company). In this traditional view, everyone else is an outsider. Vendors provide materials; the company cuts, molds, or arranges those materials into some sort of product; and then they sell it to customers. Repeat that process as many times as possible, it goes, and you may become rich. This way of thinking makes a company the central player in a three-person chain. It is a linear approach that, even today, describes how many managers think. (See Appendix D, "Traditional View.") The manager's job is to manage vendor expectations on one side and then customer expectations on the other. They try to keep each group happy but don't spend much time thinking about how the welfare of one affects the welfare of another or how the welfare of either affects the larger community.

The Market Basket case illustrates an emerging view that is quite different and still somewhat controversial. People at Market Basket have a starkly different view of who is inside and who is outside. Based on Arthur T.'s principle of reciprocal loyalty, insiders are those who fully subscribe to the company's purpose. One becomes an insider at Market Basket not by taking a job or getting a new title but by earning it, preferably over time.

Moreover, associates know that many customers have shopped for generations and share their values. These customers are invited into the extended family of Market Basket. As Robert Mnookin, a Harvard Negotiation Research Project chair, told WGBH Boston, "Indeed, a lot of the customers of this grocery chain felt like they were part of the family. That family culture was terrific." We see the same thing for select vendors. Vendors who have worked with Market Basket buyers for years and who share values with others at the company become part of the family. It becomes a relationship that transcends the day-to-day deliveries, invoices, and payments of the business. Community members often feel the same sort of connectedness to the company. Even many who don't shop there have friends who work at Market Basket and know how many decent-paying retail jobs it creates.

But James Post, the Boston University professor we've heard from throughout this book, argues that this approach is too simplistic. He says, "Your job as an executive, as a CEO, or a senior executive is to understand how all these relationships contribute to a firm's success and to be imaginative and positive in how you manage all those relationships." Market Basket seems to appreciate these connections more than most. It does so well because its success depends on how well this virtuous cycle is humming. Vendors are constantly reminded that they are providing a service to customers. Customers believe that their purchases are supporting a business that gives good jobs in the community.

All these stakeholders (employees, customers, vendors, and the community) work together as a network, not a linear process. (See Appendix D, "Market Basket View.") If you were to ask a loyal employee, customer, or vendor, "who is Market Basket," they might draw something like this: Arthur T., associates, vendors, customers, the community, and perhaps the B directors on the board are considered insiders, working together and each contributing to grow the business and each other's welfare.

But woe to those who threaten the Market Basket family or its way of doing things. No matter what contractual right they think they have, "family" members will consider them to be outsiders. Before and during the protest, A directors, including Arthur S., some of the other shareholders, and the new CEOs (who replaced Arthur T.), were viewed as separate and in opposition to the Market Basket family. As we saw during the protest, the relationship between family members and these outsiders became downright adversarial.

Pundits were surprised at just how broad the coalition of the protest was. Associates, managers, customers, and vendors were all working together. Under the traditional view, it should have been easy for the new CEOs to exploit potential fissures between these groups—to simply find areas in which their self-interest diverged and try to pit one subgroup against another.

This was a family that had been born over time. Unity had been forged through years, in some cases decades, of proving one's loyalty, even under hardship. Individuals acted as much on behalf of this extended family as their self-interest. Such a unity is not easy to break. The fissures are less obvious. The only way to break such a group is to convince members that the ideal they are fighting for is the wrong one.

Others—like the media, academics, and government officials—are viewed in more neutral terms; any individual within those groups might be considered an insider or an outsider depending on his or her public or private stance on the Market Basket dispute.

What we see at Market Basket is a more nuanced and psychological sense of who is part of the company and who isn't. During the protest, the replacement CEOs and the directors who were loyal to Arthur S. were considered outsiders, while the ousted CEO and shareholders loyal to him were considered part of the family. There are no prefabricated notions of who belongs; it is a company in which lines were drawn based on people's loyalty.

—

Market Basket should be a wake-up call to companies everywhere. But we should be careful too. The lesson is not to be more like Market Basket. Yes, the Market Basket culture is in some respects enviable, but trying to emulate it would be misguided.

Rather than trying to become more like Market Basket or some other prototype, companies need to become better at being themselves. What companies need to do is dig deeper into who they are and how they can serve others better. It is what some are calling "corporate purpose." That purpose is a company's reason for being.

To capture what that means for your organization, a thought experiment might help. Ask yourself what would happen if the organization you work for were to suddenly disappear—if the CEO and top managers were to fade away and any stores or buildings that the organization occupies were to empty out in the blink of an eye.

Would anyone notice?

For too many companies, the answer is "not really." People would simply find a similar company to work for or purchase from. Many companies are successful in terms of financial performance. Much fewer are successful in making a difference in people's lives that others cannot imitate.

Even after reading this book, some readers may argue that corporate purpose is a nice idea but that when it comes down to it, only money talks. We would argue that money can be a powerful incentive, but it is not the only one and is not always the most powerful. Consider the fact that the CEO of Victory Supermarket tried to woo Market Basket employees for years; he was never successful. Consider the lengths to which customers went to avoid shopping at Market Basket, even though they knew they would have to pay more for groceries elsewhere. Consider the vendors who risked their livelihoods by stopping shipments to Market Basket.

As venture capitalist Anthony Tjan wrote in a blog for the *Harvard Business Review*, "It turns out there are many ways to make a billion dollars: real estate, investing, gaming and entertainment, retail, technology, and good old-fashioned inheritance. But the most interesting (and most respected) businesses and personalities are also the ones with the strongest and most authentic purposes behind them."

As we have seen throughout this book, people are sometimes willing to make personal sacrifices if they believe that they are contributing to something that is larger than themselves. In Market Basket's case, that something is its extended family across New England.

Uncovering this purpose is not just an exercise for executives; we have argued in this book that Market Basket's culture is behind the extraordinary movement that reinstated their CEO and saved a beloved business. That culture was fostered by senior executives for years, but it was also shaped by everyone in the company. If we accept this, then we must realize that such a purpose cannot be imposed by executives. It must be something constructed by people who care about the organization.

Each company will have its own culture and purpose based on its unique history and relationships with people. Market Basket has its own reason for being and so should Shaw's, Hannaford, and all its other competitors. Without understanding what they stand for and why they need to exist, they run the risk of being just some of many choices vying for attention in a crowded marketplace. That does not give employees a meaning to strive for, customers something to cheer for, or vendors a goal to work toward.

The Market Basket case is reason for pause. Too often, we forget why we are in business and whom we are trying to serve. Those simple questions do not have simple answers, but they *are* worthwhile. Those courageous enough to grapple with them may be rewarded not only with good performance but also with the fulfillment that comes with meaningful work.

EPILOGUE

At the time of writing, Market Basket is not only back on its feet but thriving. The fall of 2014 saw new store openings. Five new Market Baskets opened by February 2015. Each opening was a tremendous success, with sales outpacing original estimates. Managers say they are going to catch their breath for a time before opening more.

Market Basket today retains much of the character it had before the protest. Shoppers continue to clog the aisles looking for bargains. Teenagers still circle the parking lots "shagging" shopping carriages. By now, almost all the signs from the protest have been removed from the walls inside stores (although one or two remain back in the loading areas of many stores). To see a Market Basket today is not unlike seeing it before the protest.

But something in the air is different.

The memories may be fading, but a certain brand of pride remains. Those who protested feel that they were part of something important, even historic. They hope that their actions will inspire others to take similar actions if necessary. They are heartened that their story has attracted national attention. In November, Secretary of Labor Thomas Perez opened his hour-long remarks at the National Press Club with the Market Basket story. "They really have captured the imagination of the nation," he said.

Associates, customers, vendors, lawmakers, and community members all banding together to save a beloved business and its culture is unprecedented. Experts believe that this will be studied in business schools for years.

Arthur T.'s status in the region has changed. He is now not only recognized but revered by thousands, if not millions. "He's a rock star," says Linda Kulis, accounts receivable supervisor. She told of a recent visit to store #43 in Nashua. He made the trip unannounced, "so he could get in and get out, but he was there for three and a half hours, greeting people, signing autographs." She says nowadays, "Everyone wants to meet him."

Others have been affected on a more personal level. You may recall the story of Karla Foster helping an elderly woman shop every Friday morning. Foster did not know her name, but she helped the woman find products and even choose greeting cards for loved ones. "If I didn't see her for a week, I would worry, but then I would see her the next week, and I'd be grateful," she recalls. Tears begin to form in Foster's eyes. "I have not seen her since we came back. And it breaks my heart because I don't know if something happened to her. I don't know her name." Thinking back to the protest reminds her of that woman and also of the others she serves.

For some, there are also the sudden, unexpected reminders of the protest. Barbara Paquette says that before the protest, she might have seen a news story about a company in crisis or people picketing and "not have looked twice." Now she empathizes. She says she "looks at things differently now" and takes a lot less for granted. Even as she goes through her daily routines at work, she rarely makes snap decisions superficially; she "look[s] at everything more closely" to see how her decisions will affect other people. Like so many associates at Market Basket, Paquette is proud of the role she played in the protest. "I feel very good about what I did," she says. "I sleep good every night; I would do it again in a heartbeat."

Store Director Mark Lemieux still says, "I'll tell you one thing: I feel good. We fought the good fight. There was one person in the world

Arthur S. didn't want to sell to, and it was Arthur T. And we made him do it." It's not unusual to hear vendors and customers say similar things.

Tim Malley, the vendor who wrote the open letter toward the end of the 2014 protest, says it was "one of the best things [he] ever did."

Many of these associates, customers, and vendors look back on the protest as a transformative experience. It is rare that the opportunity comes along to stand up for something one believes in. It is just as rare for such a diverse group of people, unified by their loyalty to a man and their love for a company, to come together and seize that opportunity.

Bill Marsden, the senior executive who was fired along with Arthur T. and has now returned as a key advisor, sums it up this way: "We're a rich company, but it's not because of the money; it's because of the people." He says that their belief in each other and in the company gave them a strength that the board and others could not match:

"We're a tough bunch. They didn't stand a chance from day one."

AUTHORS' NOTE

This book grew out of conversations between the two authors back in 2013. By that time, the board of directors was trying to fire its CEO. That alone would not be terribly newsworthy; after all, the tenures of CEOs have gotten shorter over the years. But something very different was happening here. Thousands of people were demonstrating to keep Arthur T. Demoulas as Market Basket's CEO. Adding to the drama, the upcoming board vote to fire Mr. Demoulas stemmed from a family dispute that went back more than two decades and involved some of the largest and most hotly contested lawsuits in Massachusetts history.

One author (Welker) was covering the Market Basket story for the *Lowell Sun*. The *Sun* has a long and storied history, but it has a small newsroom compared to heavyweights, like the *Boston Globe*. This also offered Welker an opportunity. He could fully immerse himself in the story, covering it from every angle.

The other author (Korschun) was drawn to the Market Basket story for academic reasons. He was already very familiar with Market Basket from more than twenty years of living in Massachusetts and New Hampshire. But the story was intriguing because it seemed to capture, in a single case study, many of the concepts he had been arguing for years in academic papers.

We continued on our separate work for almost a year—Welker on his reporting and Korschun on a case study he was developing for his executive master of business administration course on Corporate Social

Responsibility. It was not until we were contacted by our editor, Stephen Power, in mid-August 2014 that we began to consider joining forces to tell the story as a book. Power had been following the protest from his office in New York City and agreed with us that the dramatic events unfolding in New England needed to be told to a wider audience.

The coverage at the *Sun* and *Globe*, as well as other newspapers, radio stations, and television outlets, was generally excellent. The daily stories captured all the daily events and often provided perspective through expert analysis. But no single article could quite capture the grassroots movement that was growing to include millions of people across New England.

We all agreed that a book was necessary to do justice to the story. Furthermore, we felt that writing it together, from both journalistic and academic perspectives, would draw out additional insights for us and for readers.

We began our investigation by scouring everything that had been written about Market Basket over the years. Then, once the deal was closed on December 12, 2014, some company insiders were gracious enough to tell us their stories. We remain grateful for their trust. We spoke first with senior managers at Market Basket who spearheaded the movement, spiraling out from there to include associates in other functions, as well as customers, lawmakers, vendors, and others. We hoped to include the perspective of Arthur T. himself. He declined to be interviewed for this book.

Although our primary interest was understanding how the movement grew, we also wished to include the perspectives of those who opposed the movement. We reached out to key players among that group. We attempted to contact replacement CEOs Felicia Thornton and James Gooch. They declined to comment. We also made multiple calls to the public relations firm that represented some members of the board (Kekst and Company). Those calls were never returned. Individual directors also declined to comment on the record.

To reach the widest audience possible, we decided to give the writing a conversational tone. That tone is also reflective of the down-to-earth nature of Market Basket. We want readers to experience the company as we did: as one person recounting the story to another person.

APPENDICES

Appendix A: Arthur T. Spars with
Arthur S. and Gerrard Levins in 2012

Arthur T.: This is running the business and treating the people the way they should be treated and running the business the way it should be run. That's my reference to this extraordinary bonus that we anticipate, and we'll put our Ps and Qs together and do the right thing.

Arthur S.: When do you think it's going to be in 2010?

Arthur T.: I would say it would be third or fourth quarter.

Arthur S.: And what do you think it's going to—what do you anticipate it to be?

Arthur T.: I don't know yet.

Arthur S.: Do you have any clue whatsoever?

Arthur T.: It will be substantial. I would say in the $20 million to $40 million range.

Arthur S.: And so that's above and beyond what the other one was or 20 to 40—

Arthur T.: Which other one? Referring to the one last June, the $2.7 million one?

Arthur S.: The normal bonus.

Arthur T.: The extraordinary is above and beyond the December bonus and above and beyond the March bonus.

Arthur S.: So next third or fourth quarter, whatever bonuses they normally get—

Arthur T.: This is above and beyond that.

Arthur S.: It would be $20 to $40 million above that?

Arthur T.: That's correct. The details aren't ironed out yet. The timetable's not committed yet. Is it 100 percent that we're going to do it? It's not 100 percent, but it's on our radar screen.

Gerard Levins: Just one follow-up. When would the board find out that it's definitive? The reason I bring it up is because last year I didn't think it was $20 million. Now it's $20 to $40 million. We're contributing $40 million-plus to the profit-sharing plan this year, based on performance and everything that you mentioned earlier. And now it sounds like this has potentially doubled, and it's going to be at your discretion and management's discretion.

Arthur T.: That's correct.

Gerard Levins: And so my question is: When does the board find out that it's going to go forward?

Arthur T.: Probably the first meeting after it happens.

Arthur S.: After it happens?

Arthur T.: Right.

Arthur S.: Not before? You're not going to talk about it before with the board?

Arthur T.: Are you looking for notification, or are you looking to have approval from the board?

Arthur S.: We're looking for notification and justification and what the reasons are.

Arthur T.: Well, I just gave you the reasons; and if you're looking for notification, we'll consider letting the board know before it happens. If not, we'll let you know right after it happens.

Arthur S.: Well, it's his job to inform the board; and it's his job to inform the board beforehand, not after it's done. It's extraordinary. It's an extra $20 million or $40 million.

Arthur T.: I want to tell you, Arthur, you hired me to run the company, OK; and when you hired me, you hired my management style. And my management style, OK, is to do what's in the best interests of Demoulas Super Markets, OK, on any topic that I believe we're doing that's in the best interests of Demoulas Super Markets, OK. And my management style is not to come back to this board to request and ask for permission. I'm going to do it . . .

Appendix B: Arthur S. Spars with William Shea at Board Meeting in 2003

Arthur S.: So whatever complaints somebody has, I agree with you. Put them in writing, spell them out from A to Z. And if they have any complaints about me and my behavior, highlight them.

Shea: People have said that, they have a problem with your behavior and that comes from—

Arthur S.: Well, I have a problem with your behavior, and I have a problem with Sumner Darman's behavior, and I have a problem with Carleton's behavior.

Shea: And I want to—

Arthur S.: And you know something? And I am sitting here doing what is best for the company.

Shea: And I want to—

Arthur S.: So if someone wants to find fault, OK, let him come out and do it.

Shea: And I want to put it on the record, and if someone complains, I want it in writing.

Arthur S.: You know what, Mr. Shea? I know what this is all about, and you know, the funny thing is we always know—

Shea: What's it all about?

Arthur S.: We always know.

Shea: What's it all about?

Arthur S.: Excuse me. Did you say, "Don't interrupt?" Were you the guy who said "Don't interrupt?" Then don't interrupt me. OK?

I see right through this. You guys have your little games you play every single meeting.

Shea: Then I'm going to challenge you not to interrupt other people.

Arthur S.: Oh, well, you do that.

Shea: How about that?

Arthur S.: You do that. That's very nice of you.

Shea: Huh?

Arthur S.: Yes.

Shea: The first time you interrupted today—

Arthur S.: I'm so threatened by you, pointing your finger at me.

Shea: The first time you interrupt today—

Arthur S.: What are you going to do?

Shea: —You're going to hear the same thing.

Arthur S.: Oh, is that right?

Shea: That's right.

Arthur S.: Oh well—

Shea: Or we'll adjourn the meeting.

Arthur S.: See, you're already threatening me.

Shea: I'm not threatening you. You threatened me.

Arthur S.: The other thing is, don't interrupt the meeting, and you color the record all you like, Mr. Shea. Color the record.

Shea: And you haven't done that for the past four or five years?

Arthur S.: Color it in your defense. Color it in your defense.

Shea: Go ahead, you got a comment, Jerry?

Levins: Yes, I do, just to follow up on what Mr. Demoulas said. Mr. Carleton started first, and he took responsibility that he participated or he was responsible for certain parts. Mr. Demoulas asked you about 20 minutes ago what the conversation was with Mr. Darman, and it was "they," "that." Now Mr. Demoulas asked you, and you said, "It was you, Mr. Demoulas." Didn't you have the guts 20 minutes ago to say that they were talking about Mr. Demoulas? Now all of a sudden, you have the guts to say, "Oh, they're talking about Mr. Demoulas?" You don't need to comment. It's on the record. You're inconsistent time and time again, and the record speaks for itself.

Arthur S.: Well, I'll tell you why he's inconsistent. Because you're a liar. That's why you're inconsistent.

Shea: Ed.

Pendergast: That was an example where there was no recognition given, and you interrupted. I think that we should all wait until we're recognized before we say something. If we can do that, perhaps we can be a little more civil about the process, and I'd appreciate if everybody, you and everyone else, would try to do that.

Arthur S.: Maybe we could be balanced in the process.

Shea: Wait a second. Arthur.

Arthur S.: He finished. He finished. Don't tell me to stop.

Shea: Are you recognized?

Arthur S.: Don't tell me to stop.

Shea: Are you recognized by the chair?

Arthur S.: What, are you going to run this like a third-grade class?

Shea: See, Arthur, this is exactly—

Arthur S.: Why don't we get on with the meeting, Mr. Shea.

Shea: No.

Arthur S.: OK. All you—

Shea: Jerry, you're recognized.

Arthur S.: You know, your complaints about me—

Shea: Jerry, you're recognized.

Arthur S.: —should be in writing to my attorney.

Shea: Stop it.

Appendix C: More Sparring at Board Meeting, June 25, 2003

Arthur S.: Don't pass it off like I don't have a right to ask you this question, and them I'm questioning whether you're working hard enough, because that's not what I'm questioning. I'm questioning why it was (down).

Lacourse: So why don't you listen to the answer? Wait a second. Why don't you listen to the answer? You asked us a specific question.

Why is (the) Concord (store's sales) down? We told you the bridge
was closed.

Arthur S.: Yeah.

Lacourse: We made that clear.

Arthur S.: Yeah.

Lacourse: We told you the ramp was closed. You couldn't get into the
store. We told you about Chelsea, the bridge was closed.

Arthur S.: So—

Shea: Hold it.

Lacourse: We made that very clear.

Arthur S.: I listened to all that.

Shea: Hold it.

Arthur S.: So you told me in 32 stores—

Lacourse: There's a reason for every move in every single store.

Arthur S.: And that's why customer counts or sales are down in all
those stores?

Lacourse: Absolutely.

Arthur S.: Always because of road construction or a bridge, right?

Lacourse: Bridge, road construction, competition, anything. Anything
counts to get a customer's—let me tell you something.

Arthur S.: Well, let me tell you something.

Shea: Hold it.

Arthur S.: So I can finish, OK?

Lacourse: Finish.

Arthur S.: I am concerned about our sales being down.

Lacourse: So am I.

Arthur S.: And if you want to tell me you're not, then you tell me
you're not. Tell me you're not. OK?

Joseph Rockwell, employee: He is concerned about it.

Shea: Hold on, guys. I mean this is—with all due respect, I mean, this is
not the way to conduct a board meeting.

Lacourse: I don't think so either.

Shea: To have the management team badgered by any member of the
board, it's just not constructive.

Arthur S.: You know I'm not badgering. I'm asking legitimate questions.

Shea: Arthur, I said you're badgering because I think that's what you're doing.

Arthur S.: Well, you know, it's always fine and dandy when Arthur gets to ask a question that Arthur can't get, OK, the answer. And how come—

Shea: Can you ask the question in a civil way so the man can answer? He's running our company.

Arthur S.: You know, your acting and your behavior—

Shea: He's running our company.

Arthur S.: —Mr. Chairman, is unbelievable.

Shea: How do you think your behavior is as a member of this board?

Arthur S.: As what?

Shea: The way you badger management.

Arthur S.: That's the reason we're having—

Shea: You disrespect these people. They're running a big company.

Arthur S.: That's your word, and let me say something else. The reason why we're having this discussion is because I brought it to the forefront, and we wouldn't be having it, because you'd be having it—

Shea: Can you have it in a civil way with the people that work hard every day?

Arthur S.: Use whatever language you'd like. Use whatever language you'd like.

Shea: Does the board want to entertain an adjournment of this meeting? I'm sick and tired of the way it's being conducted, and I resent that management is being badgered by a certain member of this board. I think it's absolutely reprehensible.

Arthur S.: I would say one thing.

Darman: I move we recess for five minutes.

Shea: No, I don't. We recessed for 15 minutes and considered whether this meeting is going to go on any longer.

Arthur S.: Before we do that, I recommend we adjourn, too, and I recommend the next time we have the meeting, we have what

Mr. Lacourse brought up that he doesn't care if someone leaves the company and goes out and competes against us, the thing that you want to vote for at that special meeting. I move that we adjourn this meeting too. And you always point the behavior and the behavior problems here at me. OK? When they have the problems at 32 stores losing customers and sales. And that's why it's being addressed, because it's brought to the forefront. But you guys want to go around and mosey around behind our backs and then bring it up the way you bring it up.

Appendix D: Who Is Market Basket?

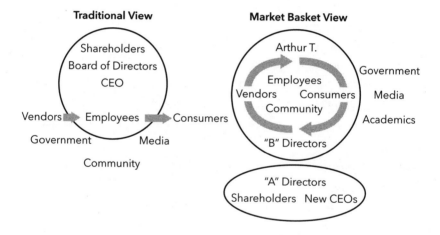

NOTES

The tone of this conflict: http://cognoscenti.wbur.org/2014/08/08/ market-basket-arthur-t-demoulas-labor-history-thomas-kochan.

Not only is the company being drained: "Pressure Mounting on Market Basket Board." By Casey Ross and Jack Newsham. *Boston Globe.* July 28, 2014.

The end game for this: http://www.wbur.org/2014/07/29/market-basket -scenarios.

The company's cash position: "Market Basket Eyes Deal This Week." By Casey Ross. *Boston Globe.* Aug. 19, 2014.

whatever cash reserve: http://www.pressherald.com/2014/08/08/ market-basket-buyer-beware-a-new-owner-would-face-significant -risks/.

By any measure, the disruption that followed: "Patrick Offers to Mediate Market Basket Donnybrook." By Casey Ross. *Boston Globe.* Aug. 9, 2014.

New Hampshire Public Radio visited: http://nhpr.org/post/how -low-are-market-basket-prices-really.

Short pay! Short pay!: http://www.lawrencehistory.org/lhcexhibits/ shortpayallout.

lots of cunning: *Lawrence and the 1912 Bread and Roses Strike.* By Robert Forrant and Susan Grabski. Arcadia Publishing, 2013. p. 8.

At first everyone predicted: http://www.massmoments.org/moment
.cfm?mid=16.

Rumor has it: "Demoulas v. Demoulas: How the Battle over a $2 Billion
Supermarket Fortune Destroyed a Family and Entangled the State's
Legal Community." By Kate Zernike. *Boston Globe.* Jan. 11, 1998.

a third of all Lowell residents: http://www.lowellhistoricalsociety.org/
research.htm.

Please remind him: *Illegit: A Memoir of Family Intrigue, Wealth, and Cruel
Indifference.* By George Demoulas. AuthorHouse, 2014.

George was president: "George Demoulas Obituary." *Boston Globe.* June 29,
1971.

It was a substantial: http://www.seacoastonline.com/article/20030525/
News/305259971.

heart disease ran in their family: "The Rich at War: Family That
Amassed Supermarket Fortune Splits in a Bitter Feud." By Joseph
Pereira. *Wall Street Journal.* July 13, 1994.

the executor of the other's estate: "The Rich at War: Family That
Amassed Supermarket Fortune Splits in a Bitter Feud." By Joseph
Pereira. *Wall Street Journal.* July 13, 1994.

cost of entry: http://www.forbes.com/forbes/2002/0415/130.html.

he established trust funds: "The Rich at War: Family That Amassed
Supermarket Fortune Splits in a Bitter Feud." By Joseph Pereira. *Wall
Street Journal.* July 13, 1994.

each month, he deposited: *Wall Street Journal.*

a lavish lifestyle for his nieces and nephews: "The Rich at War: Family
That Amassed Supermarket Fortune Splits in a Bitter Feud." By Joseph
Pereira. *Wall Street Journal.* July 13, 1994.

The venomous case: "Money Splits a Wealthy Mass. Family." By John H.
Kennedy. *Boston Globe.* Jan. 15, 1994.

There, in the Middlesex Superior courtroom: "Pawn Fights Back in
High-Stakes Arena." By Peter S. Canellos and Judy Rakowsky. *Boston
Globe.* Oct. 1, 1997.

the legal full employment act: "Demoulas v. Demoulas: How the Battle over a $2 Billion Supermarket Fortune Destroyed a Family and

Entangled the State's Legal Community." By Kate Zernike. *Boston Globe.* Jan. 11, 1998.

took a swing at his cousin: "An Inside Look at the Twists and Turns of a Legal Blood Feud." By Meghan S. Laska and Wendy L. Pfaffenbach. *Massachusetts Lawyers Weekly.* Aug. 21, 2000.

losses at $500 million to $800 million: "Demoulas' Widow Wins Suit." By John H. Kennedy. *Boston Globe.* May 27, 1994.

He was in the produce section: "The Rich at War: Family That Amassed Supermarket Fortune Splits in a Bitter Feud." By Joseph Pereira. *Wall Street Journal.* July 13, 1994.

supporter of both the church and its school: "Community Mourns a Giant." By Joyce Crane. *Boston Globe.* May 29, 2003.

It was the first time I realized: "Just One of the Boys." By Tim Lima. *Eagle-Tribune.* July 26, 2014.

Arthur T. ran for 277 yards: "The Personal Touch Cuts Both Ways with Family." By Callum Borchers. *Boston Globe.* Aug. 22, 2014.

He's that type of guy: "Just One of the Boys." By Tim Lima. *Eagle-Tribune.* July 26, 2014.

joining the board of directors: *Boston Globe.* Aug. 21, 2014.

What entrance ramp: Market Basket Board of Directors Meeting Minutes, Feb. 2, 2012.

It was the kind of thing: "Arthur S. Demoulas Shows Generosity and Resolve." By Shirley Leung. *Boston Globe.* Aug. 22, 2014.

Business scholars find: http://psycnet.apa.org/index.cfm?fa=search.displayRecord&uid=1990--97246--000.

Most corporate charters today: *The Shareholder Value Myth.* By Lynn Stout. Berrett-Koehler Publishers, 2012. p. 28.

refused to have it named after himself: "Demoulas Declines Senior Center Offer." By Christine McConville. *Boston Globe.* Mar. 13, 2003.

understand their role as corporate citizens: "Feud Makes Headlines. Philanthropy, Less So." By Grant Welker. *Lowell Sun.* Nov. 10, 2013.

will save $1.5 thousand per year: "4% Discount History, but Market Basket Shoppers Loyal." By Grant Welker. *Lowell Sun.* Dec. 31, 2014.

***Consumer Reports* ranked Market Basket**: http://www.stagnito digitalmedia.com/super50.

Market Basket is known in this community: http://www.wcvb.com/news/market-basket-deadline-day-here-return-to-work-or-be-fired/27503422.

A human being is not the son of his past: *Man's Search for Meaning*. By Victor Frankl. Beacon, 2006.

Consider the work of Adam Grant: "The Significance of Task Significance: Job Performance Effects, Relational Mechanisms, and Boundary Conditions." By Adam M. Grant. *Journal of Applied Psychology*, 93. 2008. 108.

raising consumers' standards of living: We thank Flickenberger for this wording.

How can you not be loyal: "Demoulas Feud Hits Andover Golf Club." By Grant Welker. *Lowell Sun*. June 19, 2014.

How do you begin the negotiation: Market Basket Board of Directors Meeting Minutes, Feb. 11, 2012.

I would handle Mr. Sweetser no differently: Ibid.

We're a company that likes to cultivate: http://www.bizjournals.com/boston/print-edition/2013/10/04/demoulas.html?page=2.

Psychologists realized: "Self-Categorization, Affective Commitment and Group Self-Esteem as Distinct Aspects of Social Identity in the Organization." By Massimo Bergami and Richard P. Bagozzi. *British Journal of Social Psychology*, 39. 2000. 555–577; "Identity and the Extra Mile: Relationships between Organizational Identification and Organizational Citizenship Behaviour." By Rolf van Dick, Michael W. Grojean, Oliver Christ, and Jan Wieseke. *British Journal of Management*, 17. 2006. 283–301; "Corporate Social Responsibility, Customer Orientation, and the Job Performance of Frontline Employees." By Daniel Korschun, C. B. Bhattacharya, and Scott Swain. *Journal of Marketing*, 78. 2014. 20–37.

We were always able to attract: http://www.masslive.com/news/worcester/index.ssf/2014/08/former_victory_supermarket_ceo.html.

bonuses based on company performance: "Market Basket Sale a Done Deal." By Grant Welker. *Lowell Sun*. Dec. 13, 2014.

intrinsic task motivation: *Charismatic Leadership: The Elusive Factor in Organizational Effectiveness.* By Jay A. Conger and Rabindra N. Kanungo. Jossey-Bass, 1988.

the effects of distributed leadership: "Shared Leadership in Teams: An Investigation of Antecedent Conditions and Performance." By Jay B. Carson, Paul E. Tesluk, and Jennifer A. Marrone. *Academy of Management Journal*, 50. 2007. 1217–1234.

distributed leadership can lead to dysfunction: This dysfunction involves a dispersion of responsibility (Heinicke & Bales 1953), a reduced sense of stability and security (Melnick 1982), and boundary management issues (Storey 2004).

***Harvard Business Review* accused business schools**: https://hbr.org/2005/05/how-business-schools-lost-their-way.

80/20 rule: http://www.youngupstarts.com/2011/11/04/flipping-coins-for -clv-dollars.

It handles the traffic: http://www.wbur.org/2014/07/23/market-basket -website-mystery.

The shift [of Rafaela Evans]: "A Switch in Allegiance and Market Basket Dominoes Began to Fall." By Grant Welker. *Lowell Sun.* July 27, 2014.

Banding together to remove the CEO: "The Market Basket Fairy Tale." By Holman Jenkins. *Wall Street Journal.* Sept. 27, 2014.

You wonder, why rock the boat now?: "As Dedicated Workers, Customers Sing CEO's Praises, Analysts Appear Mixed on Impact of His Possible Ouster." By Grant Welker. *Lowell Sun.* July 17, 2013.

It's very hard to build a family business: "Experts: Demoulas Fight Shows Family Business Can Be Two-Edged Sword." By Grant Welker. *Lowell Sun.* July 18, 2013.

Now if [they] don't do it, [they] waffled: Ibid.

There's only one boss: Market Basket Board of Directors Meeting Minutes, Aug. 30, 2012.

hired [his] management style: Market Basket Board of Directors Meeting Minutes, Nov. 5, 2009.

I'll never forget you: "Demoulas Seizes the Day." By Grant Welker. *Lowell Sun.* July 19, 2013.

four significant actions: "Source: Demoulas Board Seeks Executive Search Firm." By Grant Welker. *Lowell Sun*. Aug. 24, 2013.

You don't hire a search firm: "Shopping Cart Full of Changes Looming for Market Basket." By Grant Welker. *Lowell Sun*. Sept. 1, 2013.

sent a letter directly to associates: Ibid.

Fear and anger: "Market Basket Employees Respond to Letter." By Grant Welker. *Lowell Sun*. Sept. 4, 2013.

We respectfully request: "Market Basket Employees Respond to Letter." By Grant Welker. *Lowell Sun*. Sept. 4, 2013.

less drastic: "Market Basket Approves Bonuses." By Grant Welker. *Lowell Sun*. Nov. 28, 2013.

Dear Scott, Thank you: Ron Weiner. E-mail message forwarded to authors by Scott Patenaude.

The judge decided: http://caselaw.findlaw.com/ma-superior-court/1647655 .html#footnote_8.

only twenty-two Fortune 500 companies: http://fortune.com/2014/ 09/20/oracle-two-ceos-disaster.

Felicia Thornton, who was given the title: "Is Market Basket Fight Over? Don't Count on It, Analysts Say." By Grant Welker. *Lowell Sun*. June 25, 2014.

Jim Gooch was named co-CEO: Ibid.

Both had contracts that guaranteed payment: "Constant Challenges, No Certainties for New CEOs at Market Basket." By Callum Borchers. *Boston Globe*. Aug. 6, 2014.

Sterling Golf Management to take over the club's operations: "Demoulas Feud Hits Andover Golf Club." By Grant Welker. *Lowell Sun*. June 19, 2014.

We believe that while all: "Market Basket CEOs, 'Artie T.' Supporters, on Collision Course with Walkout Planned Today." By Grant Welker. *Lowell Sun*. July 18, 2014.

e-mail seemed to have galvanized them: "Market Basket Workers Play Rally for Ousted CEO." By Erin Ailworth and Jack Newsham. *Boston Globe*. July 18, 2014.

This isn't work for all of us: "Loyalty to the Ousted Demoulas." By Erin Ailworth. *Boston Globe*. July 16, 2014.

We're a crazy bunch: "Loyalty to the Ousted Demoulas." By Erin Ailworth. *Boston Globe*. July 16, 2014.

I'm so proud of [the warehouse workers]: Dean Joyce, thirty-four-year Market Basket employee, Tewksbury distribution center manager, speech at July 24, 2014, rally.

115th Old Home Day Parade: https://www.youtube.com/watch?v =bbn3V1K340A.

Merrimack Valley Food Bank was a short-term beneficiary: "Boycotting Market Basket Has Its Costs." By Grant Welker. *Lowell Sun*. July 28, 2014.

It's an introvert's paradise: "Talks Continue as Pressure Grows for Market Basket Sale." By Grant Welker. *Lowell Sun*. Aug. 20, 2014.

This company never needed: http://www.wbur.org/2014/09/03/market -basket-labor.

This is our f-ing city: http://www.huffingtonpost.com/2013/04/20/ red-sox-ceremony-david-ortiz-boston_n_3123316.html.

I have issued an immediate communication: http://www.concord monitor.com/news/13053051-95/market-basket-part-time-employees -hours-eliminated.

It's in the customer's hands: http://www.masslive.com/news/boston/ index.ssf/2014/08/thousands_rally_in_show_of_sup.html.

We want you to know: "An Open Letter to Our Customers and Communities." By Felicia Thornton and Jim Gooch. *Boston Globe*. July 19, 2014.

raised more than $20 thousand: http://www.gofundme.com/cdm2kk.

censure President Clinton: http://front.MoveOn.org/about.

The customers are the locomotive: http://www.masslive.com/news/ boston/index.ssf/2014/08/thousands_rally_in_show_of_sup.html.

red districts are getting redder: http://commonwealthmagazine.org/ politics/001-the-blue-red-color-divide-in-massachusetts.

You know, what we're dealing with here: Deval Patrick. Aug. 6, 2014. Press conference transcript provided by the Office of the Governor of Massachusetts.

held hostage to a private dispute: Deval Patrick. Aug. 13, 2014. Press conference transcript provided by the Office of the Governor of Massachusetts.

We will not go back to work: http://wearemarketbasket.com/to-be-clear.

Well, I certainly don't: Deval Patrick. Aug. 6, 2014. Press conference transcript provided by the Office of the Governor of Massachusetts.

All parties report: "Beat Goes on for Contentious Market Basket Maneuvering." By Grant Welker. *Lowell Sun.* Aug. 26, 2014.

Market Basket and its shareholders are pleased: http://www .bostonglobe.com/business/2014/08/27/statement-from-market -basket-shareholders/Gi5Z879oMhZsoJKG6Efp5I/story.html.

See you at 7 AM: http://www.latimes.com/nation/nationnow/la-na-nn -market-basket-ceo-arthur-t-demoulas-20140828-story.html.

It becomes part of your family: http://bigstory.ap.org/article/settlement -reached-supermarket-chain-feud.

As I stand before you, I am in awe: "Artie T. Makes Triumphant Return to Market Basket HQ." By Chelsea Feinstein. *Lowell Sun.* Aug. 28, 2014.

We go forward with a commitment: https://www.youtube.com/watch ?v=an8eJtnwDJ4&list=PLany35c1q3os0Ub1dMFdheBV14GWjvCs2.

McKinsey recently found: http://www.mckinsey.com/Insights/Organization/ Why_diversity_matters?cid=other-eml-alt-mip-mck-oth-1501.

all powers granted to a corporation: "Corporate Powers as Powers of Trust." By Adolf A Berle. *Harvard Law Review*, 44. 1931. 1049.

the business corporation: "For Whom Are Corporate Managers Trustees?" By E. Merrick Dodd. *Harvard Law Review*, 45. 1932. 1148.

On the face of it: http://www.ft.com/cms/s/0/294ff1f2-0f27-11de-ba10 -0000779fd2ac.html.

corporations are covered by the First Amendment: See *Citizens United v. FEC*, especially Justice Stevens, Section 1: "We have long since held that corporations are covered by the First Amendment." http://www2 .bloomberglaw.com/public/desktop/document/Citizens_United_v _Federal_Election_Commission_130_S_Ct_876_175_L_.

court extended freedom of religion rights: http://www.law.cornell .edu/supremecourt/text/13-354#writing-13-354_CONCUR_4.

Because of the legal 'personhood': http://www.princetoninfo.com/ index.php/component/us1more/?key=5-7-14stout.

A director may consider: Massachusetts Corporate Code, Part 1, Title 22, Chapter 156D, Section 8.30, General Standards for Directors.

business is under attack: "Capitalism Gets a Bad Rap, CEO Says." By Alyssa Edes. *Boston Globe*. Feb. 8, 2013.

polls that show a dismal approval rating: http://www.thedailybeast.com/ articles/2015/01/31/how-much-do-you-need-to-be-in-your-state-s-1 .html.

It turns out there are many ways: https://hbr.org/2013/09/it-takes -purpose-become-a-bill.

They really have captured: "Labor Chiefs Applauds Acts of Protesters." By Cat Zakrzewski. *Boston Globe*. Oct. 21, 2014.

INDEX